CROWOOD SPORTS GUIDES
GYMNASTICS
SKILLS · TECHNIQUES · TRAINING

Lloyd Readhead

THE CROWOOD PRESS

First published in 2011 by
The Crowood Press Ltd
Ramsbury, Marlborough
Wiltshire SN8 2HR

www.crowood.com

British Library Cataloguing-in-Publication Data
A catalogue record for this book is available from the British Library.

ISBN 978 1 84797 247 7

Disclaimer
Please note that the author and the publisher of this book do not accept any responsibility in any manner whatsoever for any damage or injury of any kind that may result from the practising, or applying, the principles, ideas, techniques and/or following the instructions/information described in this publication. Since the physical activities in this book may be too strenuous in nature for some readers to engage in safely, it is essential that a doctor be consulted before undertaking training. It is also essential that all training is supervised at all times by a qualified gymnastic coach.

Acknowledgements
The author and publisher would like to thank the following for their help in the production of this book.
Alan Edwards, for the supply of photographs.
Mark Young, for his assistance in collating the photographic images.
British Gymnastics for the use of their gymnastics library and archives.
The many gymnastic colleagues and friends who have helped the author to acquire the knowledge and experience to enable this book to be written.

Photographs © Alan Edwards Photography unless stated otherwise

Typeset by D & N Publishing, Baydon, Marlborough, Wiltshire

Printed and bound in Singapore by Craft Print International Ltd

CONTENTS

PREFACE

Gymnastics continues to grow in popularity, and there are many opportunities to participate as a gymnast, coach, judge or official. Clubs, schools and sports centres provide for all ages and abilities ranging from pre-school classes through to world and Olympic performance levels.

There are a number of gymnastic disciplines, including men's and women's artistic gymnastics, rhythmic gymnastics, acrobatics, tumbling, trampoline, double mini trampoline, aerobics, team gymnastics, freestyle and general gymnastics; more recently cheerleading has also joined the gymnastics family.

This book will concentrate on men's and women's artistic gymnastics and will aim to provide a broad understanding of these two disciplines. It will also explain how young male and female gymnasts can develop through a safe and progressive training regime.

Gymnasts are regarded as being among the fittest of all sports participants and are respected by other sportsmen and women for this, as well as their commitment and dedication. Gymnastics requires many of the qualities that athletes strive for – a gymnast must be immensely strong, superbly flexible, artistic, graceful, skilful and courageous.

The allure of gymnastics comes from the amazing number of skills and complex combination of skills that can be learnt and performed in competition routines. These offer a continuing challenge and provide the ongoing excitement for the gymnast and coach. Unlike most other sports, in gymnastics new skills continue to be invented and the rules and apparatus evolve to stimulate new ideas and ensure that the sport does not stagnate.

The book will also describe and illustrate some of the core skills that are the foundation upon which the more

advanced skills are built. Examples of current high performance skills will also be illustrated and the methods used to teach the skills described. The book should therefore be interesting for young male and female gymnasts, coaches, judges, pupils, students and parents of gymnasts.

Gymnastics must be taught in a safe and progressive manner in suitable facilities in order to facilitate learning and reduce the risk of injury. Gymnastics should only be performed in the presence of a suitably trained and qualified coach or coaches. This book is a broad guide to artistic gymnastics and is not intended to be a comprehensive training manual.

If you wish to be involved in gymnastics you should join a formally approved club or centre that uses fully qualified coaches. Details can be obtained from the national governing body for gymnastics for the particular country.

PART I
INTRODUCTION TO ARTISTIC GYMNASTICS

The Origins of the Sport

Historians have claimed that the origins of gymnastics can be traced right back to the ancient Greek and Roman civilizations, where physical exercises on various forms of apparatus were used to train the military personnel. The exercises were called 'gymnastics' and were practised in an open-air facility called a 'gymnasium'.

Some time later the Greek gymnastic exercises were modified by Guts Muths to form the basis of the German physical education curriculum. This work was further developed by Ludwig Jahn (1778–1839), who designed basic apparatus such as pommel horse, rings, parallel bars and horizontal bar, on which the exercises were practised. This lead to the formation of gymnastics clubs (*Turnvereine*) in Germany and the term 'German gymnastics' was used to refer to this form of activity. A form of men's gymnastics was included in the first modern Olympic Games in 1896 and from its origins in Europe the sport began to develop all around the world.

The first gymnastic clubs in the UK and USA were established in the 1850s. At this time the apparatus would include a pommel horse, which had a drooping end rather like a grazing horse; swinging rings; club swinging; a horizontal bar, which comprised a metal bar covered with a wooden veneer held in place by solid metal rods; and very basic floor matting, usually made from canvas covers filled with some form of coarse hair.

As more countries became involved in the sport in the early 1900s, the design of the apparatus improved and a new style of men's gymnastics evolved to form the foundation of modern gymnastics. The term 'Olympic gymnastics' was extensively used to describe the competitive form of the sport.

Women's gymnastics gained its formal international recognition at the 1952 Olympic Games and gymnasts from the Soviet Union (USSR) dominated the sport

BELOW LEFT: Skill and precision demonstrated by Beth Tweddle (GB) on asymmetric bars.

BELOW: A spectacular performance by Daniel Keating (GB) on horizontal bar.

A stylish Louis Smith (GB) on pommel horse.

Nastia Liukin. Both Canada and Australia have contended for medals but more recently the greatest surge from an English-speaking country has perhaps come from Great Britain. Beth Tweddle became Britain's first gold medal winner by becoming world champion on asymmetric bars in 2006. This was followed by a gold medal on the floor exercise at the 2009 world championships. Louis Smith won a bronze medal at the Beijing Olympics in 2008. Daniel Keatings became Great Britain's first ever European junior all-around champion just ahead of his team mate Daniel Purvis, who took the silver medal. Keatings then exceeded all expectations with a brilliant silver medal in the senior men's all-around world championship in 2009.

for over a decade. The Japanese came to the forefront of men's Olympic gymnastics in the 1960s, but the Soviet gymnasts gradually eroded the dominance of the Japanese.

In 1972 the gymnastic events at the Munich Olympics were extensively televised and the viewing audience for these events exceeded those of all the other sports. The emergence of Olga Korbut onto the world scene and the amazing performances of the other male and female gymnasts were watched by millions. The resultant boom in interest coincided with a period of growth in the building of sports centres and gymnastics facilities and together they provided the stimulus for massive growth in the sport.

At this important phase of development of the sport the more successful nations, such as the USSR, Japan, China and the Eastern European countries were employing full-time paid coaches to train the gymnasts. Many of the gymnasts were 'professional' gymnasts, who were able to train two to three times per day inside purpose-built facilities. This gave a massive advantage to these nations over those countries where gymnastics clubs were essentially volunteer, amateur organizations. Despite these disadvantages,

gymnasts from the USA and Western European countries began to appear on the medal podiums.

Up to 1970 the sport of Olympic gymnastics was predominantly for adult participants. Around this time 'talent identification and development programmes' were designed and introduced, along with training and event programmes for young gymnasts. This provided greater access to the sport and laid the foundation for more advanced and complex exercises at all levels of the sport.

Gradually more purpose-designed and dedicated gymnastics facilities were constructed and more opportunities to become full-time paid coaches were created in the Western world. The injection of state funding into gymnastic programmes in these countries led to a more level playing field and a wider range of countries are now winning world and Olympic medals in what is now called 'artistic gymnastics'.

This point may be underlined by the successes of gymnasts from the USA, who have won numerous medals at world and Olympic events. Some of best known are Kurt Thomas, Bart Conner, Paul Hann, Mary Lou Retton, Dominique Dawes and

The History of Gymnastics at the Olympic Games

The first modern Olympic Games were held in Athens, Greece in 1896. Men's gymnastics was one of seven sports included in the programme, and the first men's Olympic champion was Alfred Flatow from Germany. The men's gymnastics programme has been present in every Olympic Games since.

A form of women's gymnastics, including swinging rings, was introduced into the Olympic programme in 1928 but it was not until the 1952 Helsinki Games that the women's all-around four-piece event was introduced. The Olympic champion was Maria Gorokhouskia from the USSR.

There have been some amazing achievements at the Olympic Games. For example, the USSR held the women's team title for eight consecutive years from 1952, while the men's team from Japan won the Olympic title at five consecutive Olympic Games from 1960 to 1976. Vitali Scherbo (Belarus) holds the record for the highest number of gold medals at one Olympic Games. He claimed six gold medals at the 1992 Barcelona Games.

Both men's and women's artistic gymnastics events are included in the current Olympic Games programme and medals are awarded for the: men's team and women's team; men's and women's all-around (AA); and individual apparatus championships on vault, asymmetric bars, beam and floor exercise for women, and floor exercise, pommel horse, rings, vault, parallel bars and horizontal bar for the men. Gymnastics enjoys one of the largest television audiences of all the Olympic sports and tickets for gymnastic events at the games are frequently the first to be sold out.

LEFT: *Former Olympic champion Svetlana Khorkina from Russia.*

BELOW LEFT: *Olympic champion Jang Wei of China.*

BELOW: *A typical modern gymnastics training facility.*

Influences on the Development of Gymnastics

The modern form of artistic gymnastics has evolved over many years, and the main influences on the gradual increase in skill difficulty have been:

• Improvements in apparatus design, culminating in the modern sprung and carpeted floor area, sprung top vaulting table, dynamic springboards, fibreglass asymmetric bars and sprung steel horizontal bar. The much improved specification for landing surfaces has also added improved safety.

• The impact of sports science on coaching and training regimes, leading to incredible levels of strength and fitness in the gymnasts. Knowledge gained in biomechanics, exercise physiology, sports psychology and planning is used to design the training programmes in gymnastics.

• The evolution of the modern dedicated

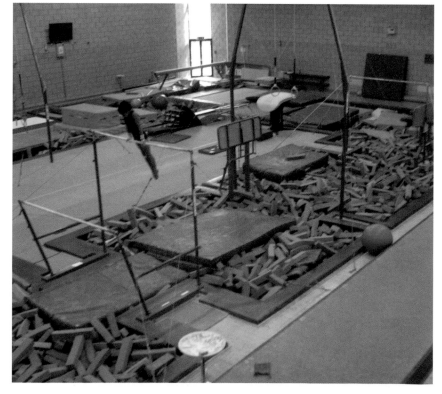

gymnastic training facility. Gyms now have pitted landing areas, better landing modules, multiple sets of each apparatus, and training aids such as trampolines sunk into the gym floor.

Key Landmarks in Gymnastics

The world governing body for gymnastics is the Fédération Internationale de Gymnastique (FIG). The FIG has traditionally reviewed its rules and regulations every four years at the conclusion of each Olympic cycle. This allows the leading experts to keep the rules in line with recent developments in performance and to ensure that new trends are accommodated or regulated.

Any new element which is performed at a major event may be named after the gymnast who first performed the skill. For example the Tkatchev is named after Alexander Tkatchev, who was the first to perform this skill on the horizontal bar. The FIG will also attach a difficulty rating to the new skill.

A Stalder circle being performed by Kohei Uchimura (Japan).

Notable Landmarks in Artistic Gymnastics

1896 – Men's artistic gymnastics included in the first modern Olympics, held in Athens.

1903 –World Gymnastics Championships created with just four teams competing in the inaugural tournament.

1948 – The 'Stalder Circle', a skill that is still extensively used on horizontal bar and asymmetric bars, first performed by the Swiss gymnast Joseph Stalder.

1952 – Women's artistic gymnastics all-around championship included for the first time in the Helsinki Olympic Games.

1964 – Sergei Diamidov demonstrates an innovative full turn around one arm into the handstand position on Parallel Bars. The Diamidov element is still popular in men's gymnastics.

1970 – Mitsuo Tsukahara (Japan) performs a round-off tucked back somersault over the vaulting horse. The Tsukahara vault is now frequently performed in the straight position by both male and female gymnasts.

1972 – The shape of the asymmetric bars altered to become round, and they are now manufactured from fibreglass to provide much greater flexibility. Around this time the FIG also introduces important modifications in the sprung floor area and competition landing modules.

1972–75 – Pommel horse exercises changed significantly. Zoltan Magyar invents a forward travel facing along the horse (the Magyar), which is then performed in a backwards direction by Janos Sivado (the Sivado Travel). Kurt Thomas from the USA performs a splits position during the circle and this spectacular and elegant skill is named the 'Thomas Flair'.

1976 – Jorge Roche (Cuba) adds a one-and-a-half front somersault to his handspring vault and the 'Roche Vault' is added to the list of vaults. A new trend is established on the horizontal bar when three new 'release and re-catch' elements are performed at the European Championships in Vilnius. These were the Tkatchev (Alexander Tkatchev, USSR), the Gienger salto (Eberhard Gienger,

Germany) and the Deltchev, performed by Stoyan Deltchev (Bulgaria).

Romanian gymnast Nadia Comaneci takes the world by storm, performing superbly at the Olympics to amass a string of perfect 10s.

1983 – Female gymnast Natalia Yurchenko (USSR) competes with a vault that includes a round-off and backward take-off from the springboard followed by a backward somersault from the hands. This inspires a new range of imaginative vaults called the Yurchenko.

1986 – The improvement in the construction of the sprung floor area allows Valeri Liukin (USSR) to perform the first triple tucked back somersault in the floor exercise. Valeri is the father of Olympic champion Nastia Liukin and is now a coach to the USA women's team.

1997 – The global trend towards younger female gymnasts becomes a real concern, and in order to protect young participants from overuse injury the FIG changes the minimum age for major events to 13 years (junior) and 16 (senior). This has the desired effect and it is now common to see mature females such as the Beth Tweddle and Svetlana Khorkina competing at the highest levels. Svetlana famously won three consecutive

ABOVE: The Tkatchev release and re-catch element.

RIGHT: Rebecca Bross (USA) mid-flight during a release and re-catch on A-bars.

ABOVE: The technique used in the Yurchenko vault.

RIGHT: Becky Downie (GB) powering off the vault during a Yurchenko vault.

women's artistic world championship all-around titles.

The FIG drops the compulsory exercises from the international programme. Prior to 1997, gymnasts competing at world and Olympic championships had to compete with both compulsory and voluntary exercises on each apparatus. This format certainly identified the best all-around gymnasts but it was a lengthy and demanding programme. It was felt that this format discriminated against gymnasts from developing countries who were not in full-time training. It was also noted that the compulsory event was not popular with the spectators or television producers, so the FIG therefore took the bold decision to drop the compulsory exercises.

2001 – A new Judging Code of Points is introduced. Scores above ten points can now be awarded and it is possible to set world best scores in each event. Typically scores of around 15.00 to 16.00 points are awarded for top-class performances on each apparatus. The Judging Code of Points will continue to evolve with frequent small changes being made to incorporate new advances and to ensure that the sport does not stagnate.

The Structure of Gymnastics

The sport of gymnastics is popular throughout the world and the rules established by the FIG, the highest authority, are usually cascaded downwards and customized to suit the needs of the particular local body. Typical areas of responsibility are shown below.

The World Governing Body for Gymnastics

The Fédération Internationale de Gymnastique (FIG) is based in Switzerland and serves to govern all aspects of the sport at international level. The elected international representatives serve on committees that each have a specific role, deciding on matters such as:

- Technical regulations for each discipline of the sport, including competition rules and judging criteria (The Judging Code of Points)
- Apparatus dimensions and design specifications
- Codes of conduct and practice for gymnasts, coaches, judges and officials
- The health and welfare of the gymnasts
- Regulations for the control of banned drugs
- The organization of major events such as the world and Olympic championships, and grand prix events.

The FIG accepts membership from recognized national governing bodies

Three times world champion – Svetlana Khorkina from Russia.

2002 – The FIG 'World Age Group Programme' for gymnastics launched. This initiative determines the most appropriate time to learn particular skills based on the age and maturity of the child. At the same time the FIG coaching academy is launched to standardize training and raise the quality of coaching throughout the world. The British Gymnastics Coach Education programme is recognized as one of the most advanced and successful programmes and BG is selected to host the first ever Level 3 World Academy course.

(NGBs) and each member agrees to accept and implement the FIG rules and regulations.

Continental Gymnastic Federations

Continental gymnastic federations such as the Americas, Austral-Asia and the European Gymnastic Federation often organize continental competitions and training events for gymnasts and coaches. Other geographical areas may also form suitable federations to aid the development of countries in that region, for example the South East Asia Gymnastics Confederation.

National Governing Bodies

Each country may have a formally recognized national governing body (NGB), which may apply for membership to the FIG. In the United Kingdom British Gymnastics (BG) is the body recognized by the FIG with regard to entry into the major events and the overall governance of the sport in Great Britain.

The national governing body will organize national championships for all disciplines of the sport, bestowing the title of national champion on the winner. Competitors for world, Olympic and other major championships will be selected by the NGB officials and the gymnasts will represent the FIG-recognized NGB at these events.

The NGB will usually provide training and competition opportunities through national squads and national age group competitions.

The regulations for national events are normally based upon the FIG rules at senior level but customized versions of the rules are used for the various younger age groups. The NGB may also take the lead on the training and qualification of coaches, judges and officials in their domain.

The NGB may have a network of regional/state associations or federations, each with its own governing body, whose functions are similar to and intrinsically linked with the role of the NGB.

School-based gymnastics is often looked after by a separate but affiliated body. For example, in the UK the British Schools Gymnastics Association organizes gymnastic events on behalf of schools.

Coaching and the Qualification Structure

Coaching in gymnastics is a highly technical and demanding role but can be hugely satisfying no matter at what level you are coaching. It is important that all coaches form their own coaching philosophy to ensure that they are coaching in the correct way and for the right reasons. This philosophy should be based on the coach's personal motivation to coach and should be influenced by their own values and beliefs as well as general good practice within the sport. The coach must ensure their coaching is always participant-centred and that they do not exploit the talents of the gymnasts merely to satisfy their own ego. The coach's aim should be to give the gymnasts the best possible opportunity to achieve their optimum level of performance while remembering that the gymnast's safety is paramount. It is also recommended that the coach regularly reflects on their coaching philosophy and frequently evaluates their coaching performance. This will ensure that the coach is delivering to the best of their ability and with the right motivation.

The attributes of a successful coach include dedication, commitment, ability to communicate, a desire to help others improve their performance, reliability and a good knowledge of the sport. The coach must also develop soft people skills and must be able to motivate and manage the gymnasts and other people who may be involved in the coaching programme.

It is not necessary for potential coaches to have been former gymnasts, and there are a number of instances where people without any personal gymnastic performance experience have become very good coaches. Former gymnasts will undoubtedly have a great deal of useful knowledge and understanding of the sport but may not necessarily be natural coaches. Some coaches have a natural gift for coaching but even the most talented coaches need to develop a wide range of skills and knowledge to become successful.

Potential coaches usually have to attend a recognized training course at the appropriate level and then pass an assessment to be accredited with the qualification. On the training course the coach will receive tuition on topics such as:

- How to coach using various styles of coaching, each designed to help the gymnasts learn effectively
- The responsibilities of a coach and the criteria for safeguarding the gymnasts
- Communication skills: the ability to communicate and explain complex information in a meaningful way using verbal, visual and kinaesthetic (learning by doing) methods
- Planning the training and event programme: how to meticulously plan, implement, monitor and evaluate the gymnast's short-term and long-term training and competition programme
- Sports science: the application of the principles of biomechanics, sports psychology and exercise physiology to increase knowledge and influence training methods
- Physical preparation: the methodology used to develop high levels of flexibility, strength, and endurance
- Teaching didactics: the methodology used to teach the various gymnastic skills through recognized safe and progressive part skills and the use of suitable training aids
- The physical and psychological development of the young gymnast
- Identification of talent and the development of early- and late-developing gymnasts.

The various topics are covered at a basic level in the introductory levels and gradually extended in depth at each progressive level of coaching. Coaches at the higher levels will possess a deep knowledge of the related topics and will have the ability to apply that knowledge to their coaching.

The British Gymnastics structure of coaching qualifications:

Level 1: Assistant coach – able to assist other more qualified coaches

Level 2: Coach – able to prepare, deliver and review sessions for a class

Level 3: Club coach – able to plan, implement and revise annual coaching programmes and take responsibility for a club and other coaches

Level 4: Performance coach – able to design, implement, and evaluate long-term coaching programmes and to coach high-performance gymnasts.

Other higher level qualifications may be available for coaches involved in high-performance specialist coaching.

There are many opportunities to become involved in coaching via private clubs, local authority/state classes, universities and school-based gymnastic clubs or classes.

Not all coaching opportunities in gymnastics are professional or paid and many are volunteer or part-time paid positions. However, as the popularity of the sport increases a greater number of paid professional coaches are being employed. As well as coaching in local facilities, coaches can progress to coaching at county/state, regional, national and international level.

The world governing body for gymnastics, the FIG, also runs its own Coaching Academy. This comprises three levels of qualification, which are delivered and assessed by FIG-appointed expert coaches:

Level 1 is aimed at countries where there is no recognized coach education programme

Level 2 is designed to meet the needs of countries where there are limited opportunities for coaches to be trained and accredited.

Level 3 is the highest level and is targeted at countries where there is a recognized, well-structured and approved coach education programme. Candidates on this course may achieve the international brevet coaching qualification,

which indicates that the coach is capable of coaching at the highest levels.

The three levels of FIG Academy qualifications are progressive and each course is supported by appropriate candidate resource materials. The coaches attending these training courses will study topics such as the age and stage of maturation and the development of the young gymnast; physical preparation, strength and flexibility; anatomy and exercise physiology; planning; psychology and the teaching of gymnastic skills.

The Academy courses are frequently supplemented by coach training programmes and courses organized and financed by the International Olympic Committee (IOC). These IOC course are normally located in areas or countries that are considered to be areas of gymnastic development and are delivered by FIG-appointed experts.

Qualifying as a Coach

The route to achieving qualifications in gymnastics coaching will vary in each country but the description below of the British Gymnastics Coach Education Programme is a typical model:

Registration Candidates must hold membership of the national governing body, and must meet any prerequisite criteria before enrolling on the appropriate course. In the UK it is also necessary to obtain an enhanced disclosure certificate from the Criminal Records Bureau to verify that the candidate is permitted to have access to children.

Attend the training course The course will cover the units or modules: Induction; Common Core Theory; Sport Specific Theory; Sport Specific Practical and Preparing for the Assessment.

Post-course guided learning The candidate will teach the new skills and knowledge under the guidance of a qualified coach or mentor. Specific tasks are covered and recorded in a coach's logbook. The coaches will also study the various resource packs that provide relevant information on each of the

theory topics at an appropriate level. The candidates will also prepare for the assessment under the guidance of their mentor coach.

Assessment The candidate's coaching ability and knowledge will be evaluated through assessment of the coach's logbook; Common Core and Sport Specific Theory examination papers and observation of the practical coaching.

Feedback and accreditation The assessor will debrief the candidate, identifying the coach's strengths and will also advise on a personal development action plan to address any weaknesses. Successful candidates will be accredited with the qualification.

Opportunities to Officiate

Gymnastic events could not function without the support of the judges, event organizers and event officials. Events ranging from club, county/state, regional, national through to world championship level require the services of a dedicated team of officials and judges.

The Role of the Judges

Judges are an essential ingredient of any gymnastic competition. The judges must appraise the gymnasts' performances and rank the gymnasts accordingly.

Judges are required to be:
- Trained and qualified to the level dictated by the status of the event
- Knowledgeable about the rules, regulations and Code of Points, which describe the requirements for gymnastic exercises on each apparatus and how they must be judged
- Be unbiased and fair in the implementation of the rules.

Judges must train and become qualified, and the level of accredited qualification will depend upon the judge's level of expertise and experience.

A panel of judges focus on the gymnast's performance.

The Structure of the Judging Qualifications

The highest authority for each discipline of the sport is the specific FIG Technical Committee. Members of this committee are elected by the FIG member countries from a list of the most experienced judges. The Technical Committee is responsible for designing and updating the rules and regulations and Code of Points for the specific discipline. The members of the Technical Committee serve as the superior jury and act as the apparatus supervisors at official FIG events and the Olympic Games. They also appoint the tutors and assessors who will be accredited to deliver the training for the international brevet judging qualification. The structure of the judging qualifications

and the level of responsibility are described below.

FIG International Brevet Judge Training and assessment must be undertaken at recognized international courses. The trainees are given tuition on the content and application of the FIG Code of Points for the specific discipline. The judges are assessed via a theory examination and a practical judging session and they must be able to demonstrate an in-depth knowledge of the rules and regulations as well as being able to accurately appraise the performance of international-class gymnasts. The highest category of brevet qualification is awarded to the judges who attain the highest marks in the theory and practical examinations and have a good degree of experience at major events.

These judges may be appointed as the head of a jury or panel of judges at major events. The lower levels of brevet judge are permitted to serve on the judging juries at international and other major events.

National Judge National judge candidates undertake similar training and assessment to the brevet judges whilst attending FIG-approved national courses. However, the pass mark is not as rigorous as for the international brevet qualification. National judges may adjudicate at national and dual international events and may be head of the jury for lower level events.

Regional/State Judge The judging qualifications below the national judge level will vary according to the structure and needs of the particular country but will generally be similar to that described below. The regional/state judge is assessed against a reduced version of the FIG Code of Points and candidates would not be expected to have such a high degree of skill, knowledge or experience as the national judge. Once qualified, the regional/state Judge may judge at regional/state events and certain graded events.

Club/Novice Judge The club or novice judge qualification is usually an introductory level, which covers the elementary rules of judging applied to novice or beginner events. This encourages people with little gymnastic experience to participate in judging and provides sufficient knowledge to cover basic level or graded competitions.

The Rules and Regulations of Gymnastics Competitions

The rules and regulations for major events are designed by the FIG and cover such topics as:

- The structure of competitions at world, Olympic and other major events. This could include individual all-around, team, or individual apparatus events

- The number of teams or individual gymnasts allowed to qualify or participate in certain events
- The apparatus design specifications
- The method by which judging panels and juries are appointed for major events.

The Judging Code of Points

In addition to the general rules and regulations, the guidelines for judging artistic gymnastic competitions are contained in the FIG's Code of Points. The Code of Points is sport-specific, with men's artistic and women's artistic each having separate versions. In recent years, however, the FIG has ensured that there is a great deal of commonality between the two codes. The primary purpose of the Code of Points is to provide an objective means of evaluating the gymnast's exercises and performances. The Code should ensure that the gymnasts can be ranked in order of best performance in any competition. The Code should also provide guidance to the gymnasts and coaches on the composition requirements of competition exercises. The full Code of Points will be applied at all major events, including the qualification event, team final, all-around final and apparatus finals, and may also apply to other senior events outside the major competitions. A reduced version of the FIG Code of Points is often used for junior events to ensure that the requirements on the younger gymnasts are not so demanding.

The Apparatus Jury

Where an event is governed by the FIG regulations the gymnast's performance will be assessed by the apparatus jury for each apparatus. The jury will be supervised by a member of the FIG Technical Committee, who may intervene to resolve a dispute. Each of the apparatus juries comprises two panels, the D jury and the E jury, each with a specific task.

D Jury This consists of two judges who determine the D score (sometimes called the start value), which marks the difficulty

and content of the exercise. Each gymnastic skill is rated according to its degree of difficulty, ranging from an A Part – the easiest – through to a G Part, the most difficult. With the exception of vault the difficulty ratings are as follows:

Part	A	B	C	D	E	F	G
Value	0.1	0.2	0.3	0.4	0.5	0.6	0.7

The D jury will add the nine (for men) or seven (for women) highest value parts to the value of the dismounting skill to determine the overall difficulty rating.

The rules on each apparatus require that the gymnast performs one skill from each of five selected groups of elements (0.5 for each group) and marks up to 2.5 maximum are allocated to this compositional component of the exercise.

The value of the difficulty rating and the compositional component are then added together to produce the D score. More difficult routines will be allocated higher D scores.

E Jury This consists of six judges who are responsible for evaluating the execution and presentation of the exercise. Deductions for errors in a performance are made by the E jury.

The E Score starts at 10.00 points and the judge will deduct for deviations from an ideal technical performance. The technical faults might include slightly bent arms or legs, lack of height, steps on landing right through to a fall. Errors are classified as small, medium or large error or major faults. The sum of the technical errors is deducted from the original 10.00 points by each judge. To calculate the final E score the highest and lowest scores of the six E jury judges are eliminated and the four remaining scores are averaged.

In addition to the D and E Juries there are assistant judges, who report all line faults and time faults to the D jury. Typical faults are stepping outside the perimeter of the floor area or exceeding the time allowed for completing the floor or beam exercises.

The final score is arrived at by adding the E score to the D score less any deductions (penalties) for line or time faults.

A judge assessing the performance of Kohei Uchimura on floor exercise.

Gymnastic routines contain very complex combinations of skills and the amount of information the judges have to consider is vast. The judge must record each performance through a system of symbols and at the same time record any deductions for technical errors and allocate a score that accurately reflects the gymnast's performance.

The Rights and Responsibilities of the Coach

During a competition, the coach may assist the gymnast in the following ways:
- Help to prepare the apparatus: adjusting the width of parallel bars; placing the

springboard for vault; placing or removing the springboard for the mount on asymmetric bars, beam or parallel bars or chalking up the bars
- Be present at the asymmetric bars, rings and horizontal bar during the performance to assist the gymnast in the event of a mishap
- In men's gymnastics the coach may lift the gymnast onto the rings and horizontal bar at the start of the exercise
- To assist or advise the gymnast during the 30 seconds available following a fall from the apparatus and between the first and second vault.

The coach also has the responsibility for ensuring that:
- They are familiar with the Code of Points and conduct themselves accordingly
- The height of the apparatus is not adjusted unless specifically agreed by the event organizer or head of the apparatus jury
- The gymnast can perform the routines safely and that risk of injury is minimized
- The gymnast is ready to perform when the head judge signifies that the judges are ready to view the performance
- The gymnast is not spoken to or assisted in any way during the performance
- The active judges are not approached in any way during the competition.

The penalty for contravening the rules are 0.3 points for behavioural violations and 0.5 points for apparatus-related violations. The penalty is deducted from the gymnast's final score by the head of the D jury.

The Rights and Responsibilities of the Gymnast

In a gymnastics event the gymnast has a right to:
- Have their performance judged fairly in accordance with the stipulations in the Code of Points

- Be assisted into the hang position on rings and horizontal bar in men's gymnastic events
- Have a spotter present at the asymmetric bars, rings and horizontal bar
- Rest or recuperate for 30 seconds following a fall from the apparatus (10 seconds for beam)
- Use magnesium, make adjustments to personal equipment, and confer with the coach during the allowed 30 seconds following a fall or between the two vaults
- Wear bandages, hand guards and other reasonable protective clothing
- Have a timed warm-up on each apparatus immediately prior to the competition session. This may vary according to the type of event
- Receive a conspicuous signal from the head judge (usually the raising of the right arm or a green light) 30 seconds before the exercise is expected to begin
- Repeat the exercise if it has been interrupted for reasons outside the control or responsibility of the gymnast
- Have the score publicly displayed immediately following the performance.

The gymnast has the responsibility to abide by the following regulations:
- Be attired according to the rules of the competition
- Ensure that any bandages, hand guards or other protective clothing are in good repair and do not detract from the aesthetics of the performance
- Refrain from adjusting the height of the apparatus
- Refrain from speaking to active judges during the event
- Behave in a sportsmanlike manner at all times and not distract fellow competitors
- Be ready to perform when the head judge signifies that the judges are ready to view the performance
- Raise the right arm before commencing the routine to acknowledge the judges and indicate readiness to begin performance
- Following a fall from the apparatus,

signify to the head judge that they are about to recommence the performance before remounting the apparatus
- At the end of the routine the gymnast must turn to the master judge and raise the right arm in a dignified manner to indicate that the routine is ended and to acknowledge the judge.

Different Types of Competition

At the major events such as the world championships and the Olympic Games there are four types of competition:

Qualification Event Each of the gymnasts must perform their routines on the apparatus in which they seek to qualify for the later events. The male gymnasts must perform on all six apparatus and the females on all four apparatus if they wish to qualify for the all-around final.

Team Event The top twelve teams (for men) or the top eight teams (for women) qualify from the qualification event. Usually a team comprises six gymnasts, with a maximum of five competing on each apparatus; the best four scores on each apparatus are added to produce the team's total score. The composition of the team and the number of scores counting may vary according to the rules of the particular event.

All-Around Event Usually the top twenty-four gymnasts qualify for the all-around final. The gymnasts each perform on all the apparatus (six for men and four for women) and the best combined total will determine the all-around champion. A maximum of two gymnasts from each country can compete in the all-around final. This is the most prestigious title and the one most coveted by the gymnasts.

Individual Apparatus Final Event The top eight gymnasts on each apparatus in the qualification event qualify to compete in the individual apparatus finals. The order of competing is determined by drawing lots. The gymnast gaining the highest score in the final becomes the champion on that apparatus. Often the specialist gymnasts who concentrate on just a few apparatus are the top gymnasts in these events.

The Regulations for Each Apparatus

The sequence of apparatus at gymnastic events is normally vault, asymmetric bars, beam and floor exercise for women; and floor exercise, pommel horse, rings, vault, parallel bars and horizontal bar for men.

Each apparatus is represented by a symbol on the electronic scoring system and in the event programmes. The basic rules and regulations for each apparatus are described below.

Floor Exercise (Men and Women)

The floor area measures 12m by 12m with a 1m-wide safety border. It is constructed as a sprung floor covered with a padded carpet. This provides an elastic base to allow a powerful take-off and a suitable surface to soften the impact of landing.

Performance Criteria for Women's Gymnastics
- The maximum length of a floor routine is 90 seconds.
- The exercise is accompanied by music, which may not include words.
- The routine must include a variety of tumbling and acrobatic elements connected with dance movements.
- The whole floor area should be used, and the mood, tempo and direction of the exercises should vary.
- The music, gymnastic skills and dance elements are chosen to suit the personality and style of the gymnast.

Performance Criteria for Men's Gymnastics
- The duration of the men's floor exercise is 50–70 seconds.
- The routine must include tumbling (somersaults and twists), strength and balance elements.
- The whole area must be used and personal expression adds to the variety.

In both men's and women's floor exercise points will be deducted for time violations and for stepping out of the floor area.

Marian Dragulescu (Romania), a world champion on floor exercise.

Jo Hyunjoo (Korea) leaps high on floor.

Vault (Men and Women)

The traditional vaulting horse was replaced by the vaulting table in 2001. The table is a curved, sprung and padded platform, a construction that allows great force and height to be generated from the table. The height of the table from the floor is 1.25m for women and 1.35m for men.

The maximum permitted run-up is 25m and the run-up area is covered with a carpet. The padded landing area is marked with two lines and the gymnast is required to land between these lines.

Vaulting is evaluated differently to other apparatus in that each vault is awarded a tariff according to its difficulty. The gymnast must declare the vault they intend to perform and the D panel of judges will confirm that the correct vault was executed.

The E panel will evaluate the vault by considering the height, length, body shape, exactness of turns and the control on landing between the two marked lines on the landing area.

Performance Criteria

- Gymnasts perform only one vault in the qualification and all-around competition unless they are attempting to qualify for the vault final. In this case the gymnast must perform two different vaults with different take-off or repulsion phases either forwards or backwards.
- In the vault finals the scores of the two vaults are averaged to determine the winner.

Asymmetric Bars (Women)

The measurement from the floor to the low bar is 170cm and to the high bar 250cm (plus or minus 1cm). The maximum permitted width between the bars is 180cm.

Marian Dragulescu (Romania) somersaults high above the vaulting table.

He Kexinn of China shows great skill on asymmetric bars.

Performance Criteria

- The exercise should include swinging and continuous movements in both directions, above, below and between the bars.
- Elements with twists and somersaults with multiple grip changes and flight should be included to maximize scores.
- A dismount which is commensurate with the routine must end the exercise.

Balance Beam (Women)

The beam is 10cm wide, 5m long and stands 125cm from the floor. A springboard may be used to mount the beam.

Performance Criteria

- The routine must show combinations of acrobatic elements, leaps, jumps and turns artistically linked together.
- The gymnast must work at varying levels, both close to and leaving the beam.
- The entire length of the beam must be used, and flexibility, balance and control must be shown.
- The dismount may be a forward or backward somersault or double somersault with or without twist performed from a run or a series of acrobatic elements.
- The maximum duration of the routine is 90 seconds.

Pommel Horse or Side Horse (Men)

The length of the pommel horse is 1.6m and the height from the top of the matting is 1.05m. The gymnast may adjust the width of the handles to between 40 and 45cm.

Performance Criteria

- The routine must show combinations of double leg circles, scissors and undercut circles without stops.
- All parts of the horse and handles must be used.

ABOVE RIGHT: Linlin Deng (China) going for gold on the beam.

RIGHT: A master on pommel horse – Hongtao Zhang of China.

• Swings into handstand must be smooth and without interruption or visible strength.

Rings (Men)

The rings are suspended from the ring frame, which is 5.75m high. The rings are 50cm apart and are 2.6m above the 20cm-thick landing mat.

Performance Criteria
• The routine should include strength, balance and support elements together with swinging movements in both a forwards and backwards direction.

• The routine should finish with an acrobatic dismount commensurate with the difficulty of the routine.

Parallel Bars (Men)

The bars are 3.5m long and 1.8m from the top of the landing mat. The width of the bars is adjustable from 42cm to 52cm.

Performance Criteria
• The exercise should be constructed primarily of swinging elements.
• The gymnast must work along, above and below the bars and may also work sideways across the bars.

• An acrobatic dismount must conclude the routine.

Horizontal Bar (Men)

The bar is constructed from high tensile steel 28mm in diameter. It is 2.4m long and stands 2.8m above the floor. The depth of the landing mat is 20cm, with an additional 10cm soft landing pad on top to absorb the impact of landing.

Performance Criteria
• Gymnasts are required to demonstrate continuous swinging elements in both the forwards and backwards direction.
• A release and re-grasp element and changes of grip must also be shown.
  • The routine must end with a dynamic acrobatic dismount.

LEFT: Amazing strength demonstrated on rings by Oleksandr Vorobiov of Ukraine.

BELOW LEFT: Ephe Zonderland (Netherlands) in flight above the parallel bars.

BELOW: Kohei Uchimura (Japan) high above the bar in a release and re-catch skill.

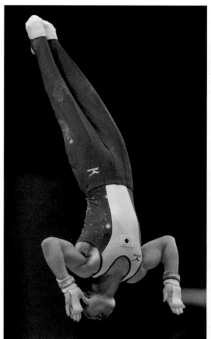

PART 2

THE DEVELOPMENT OF A GYMNAST

The Gymnast Profile

There are many inter-related qualities and attributes that contribute to the profile of a successful gymnast. The main factors are:

Natural talent A natural ability to learn many gymnastic skills and an extraordinary level of spatial awareness.
Physical attributes Suitably proportioned lean and muscular body shape, with good flexibility, strength, power, endurance, balance and excellent co-ordination.
Psychological profile High self-esteem, self-confidence, control over anxiety, a willingness to work hard, high fear threshold, courage, great commitment and, perhaps most importantly, determination and dedication.

Not all of these attributes will be overtly evident in the young gymnast as they commence their gymnastics training. Some may develop naturally over time and others can be learned through a suitable, well-structured training programme.

Talent Identification and Development

In the early stages of gymnastics participation the main features should be the all-round development of basic movement skills, balance, co-ordination and confidence. For young children their first experience of gymnastics should be enjoyable, in a fun environment that stimulates their imagination and enhances learning.

Talent detection normally occurs between the ages of five and seven for girls and six and eight for boys. The more able gymnasts who show a natural talent at learning the basic skills more quickly may be given the opportunity for more specialized training in the fundamentals of gymnastics.

Gymnastics may be classified as an early specialization sport but even so talent selection as such would not normally commence until six to eight years for girls

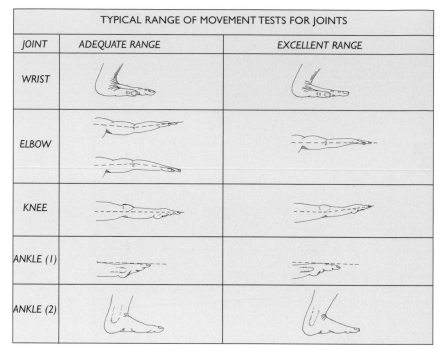

Typical range of movement tests for the gymnast's joints.

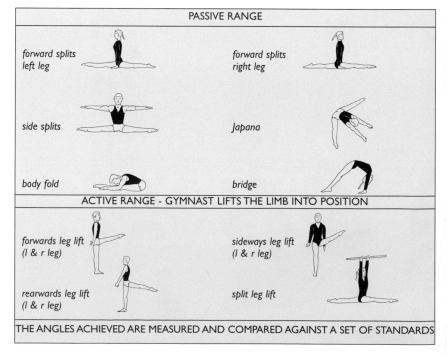

The gymnast's flexibility can be assessed using these tests.

and between seven to nine years for boys. Talent selection field tests have been graded according to the age and stage of maturation of the gymnasts and take into account the physical development, accelerated growth periods and psychological development of the growing child. The age and stage of maturation guidelines and the safe all-round development of the young gymnast is paramount in all aspects of the structured development programme.

The bank of field tests are based upon the identified norms that a 'talented' young gymnast might be expected to achieve at each stage in their development. The field tests will include exercises and activities to measure and evaluate the following:

- The competence and quality in performance of a range of essential core gymnastic skills (technical skills)
- Competition performance on each apparatus (competition performance)
- Body shape, posture, alignment of limbs and degree of range of movement in the wrists, knees, elbows and ankles (morphological measurements)
- Flexibility (both passive and active), strength, speed, power and endurance (physical preparation)
- Psychological attributes such as self-esteem, confidence and fear threshold (psychological factors).

The degree of talent identification and methods used to develop young gymnasts will vary according to the culture and structure within each country but the examples given below provide a good indication of the type of tests that are widely used throughout the world.

The angles achieved are measured and compared against a set of standards.

The Development of the Talented Young Gymnast

The physical profile tests are frequently used to assess the gymnast's profile at each stage of their development. Account will be taken of those children who may be early or late developers since there are many instances where successful gymnasts have been late in their physical and psychological development.

The talent selection programme can identify precocious talented young gymnasts, but the coach must resist the temptation to accelerate or exploit the technical development of these gifted

SOME TYPICAL PHYSICAL PROFILE STRENGTH TESTS						
DESCRIPTION	DIAGRAM	AGE AND STAGE OF MATURATION				
			8–10yrs	11–12yrs	13–14yrs	15+yrs
20 metre sprint (seconds)		f	4.3–4.5	3.6–3.8	3.4–3.6	3.2–3.3
		m	4.0–4.5	3.9–4.3	3.7–4.1	3.1–3.6
standing long jump (centimetres)		f	140–145	165–170	205–220	220–225
		m	145–155	150–160	235–245	250–270
standing vertical jump (centimetres)		f	30–35	35–38	40–45	45–50
		m	30–35	36–40	45–50	50–55
pull ups (number in 10 seconds)		f	6–8	8–10	12–14	12–14
		m	7–10	9–12	13–15	13–15
rope climb (4 metre in seconds)		f	00	8–10	6–7.5	5–6
		m	00	8–9	5.5–6.0	4.5–5.0
lift to handstand (maximum number)		f	1–2	2–3	5–7	8–10
		m	1–2	3–4	5–8	8–10
Russian lever/Manna (maximum seconds)		f	00	3–5	6–8	8–10
		m	00	3–5	6–8	8–10
horizontal rear-hang (maximum seconds)		f	00	3–5	8–10	12–15
		m	00	6–8	9–12	13–15
leg raisers (maximum number)		f	3–5	8–10	10–12	10–12
		m	3–5	8–10	10–12	10–12
rearward leg lifts (maximum in 15 seconds)		f	15–18	16–20	8–10	8–10
		m	15–18	16–20	10–12	10–12

children. They will undoubtedly learn skills very quickly but there is a danger of them reaching a plateau in their learning due to a lull in their physical and psychological development, and motivation may be lost. There is also a risk of overuse injury to the young body and a high potential for early burnout. To avoid this, the emphasis should be placed on the perfection of a wider range of skills and combination of elements so that the rate of progress is in tune with the child's physical and psychological maturation state. The aim of all good coaches should be to nurture gymnasts of varying natural ability, to attain the individual's optimum level of performance as a mature gymnast rather than produce a child superstar who may be lost prematurely from the sport.

The results of the tests are used to tailor the individual gymnast's training programme to ensure that their strengths are built upon and weaknesses are addressed and eliminated.

The thorough and caring coach will ensure that the training programme focuses on the technical, physical and psychological components with the appropriate level of intensity. It is important for the coach to take a holistic approach to their coaching to develop the gymnast's characteristics, personality, social skills and gymnastics prowess whilst still making their safety and well-being a priority.

The Key Elements of the Development Programme

Most people can participate in some form of gymnastics but the level of attainment is determined by their gymnastic ability, flexibility, strength, physical size and shape. It is important that at all levels of participation an appropriate level of physical fitness precedes the learning of gymnastics skills. In some sports it is possible to play that sport to become fit but in gymnastics the risk of injury increases and the ability to learn safely reduces if the participant is insufficiently fit. A comprehensive physical preparation programme is therefore essential for all

levels of competitive gymnastics. Indeed, this is one of key aspects of the gymnastic development programme, along with a progressive technical programme and meticulously planned event and training programme. The purpose and content of each of these components is described below.

The Physical Preparation Programme (PPP)

The purpose of the PPP is to ensure that the gymnast is sufficiently fit to embark on the skills and routine learning programme with minimum risk of injury and maximum potential for learning. The PPP should consist of:

Flexibility training The possession of good range of movement will improve the ability to learn certain skills, may reduce the risk of injury and will permit amplitude in movement to be expressed.

Strength training The various aspects of strength include static strength for held parts and balances; dynamic strength for swinging elements and lifts into handstand; and speed and power strength to enable the explosive skills to be performed.

Endurance training Gymnastics skills and exercises are learnt and perfected through the performance of many repetitions of the skills or exercises. Strength endurance is necessary to permit the many repetitions of a skill, combination of skills or routine to be performed without fatigue setting in. The onset of fatigue will reduce performance levels and may increase the risk of injury.

Most gymnastic training is anaerobic in nature, using energy stored within the muscles to sustain the short bursts of high-intensity exercise. However, aerobic endurance, where oxygen intake is essential to facilitate the energy release systems for longer bouts of lower-intensity exercise, underpins all other aspects of fitness. Aerobic endurance is required for the repetitive performance of full competition routines. This aspect of physical preparation is often neglected and undervalued by less informed coaches and must be developed early on in the annual training programme.

The Psychological Skills Programme

Often the key difference between the top gymnasts or sports people and the less successful is the ability to prepare mentally for an event or to cope with the stress or anxiety of an event. The more successful the gymnast becomes the greater the expectations become. The current champion will be tipped to win again and the media, coaches, parents, people within the sport, fellow competitors and the gymnast themselves will tend to pile on the pressure of expectation to succeed. The experienced gymnast can utilize sports psychology techniques to learn how to mentally prepare for an event and develop coping strategies to deal with the pressure. The gymnast can also learn how to utilize positive thoughts to enhance confidence and block out negative thoughts, and develop skills to mentally rehearse a skill, routine or performance in the competition arena.

Progressive Learning

The majority of even the most complex gymnastic elements are based upon a solid foundation of the core gymnastic skills. The core skills are then developed through safe progressive skills or combinations of the skills to produce the more advanced elements. A proven coaching method consists of:

- Perfection of relevant core skills (foundation skills)
- Learning safe and progressive drills and part skills to develop awareness and understanding of the movement patterns
- Linking together part skills to produce the whole skill
- Perfection of the full skill
- Combinations of individual skills
- Building up and practising part and full competition exercises.

At each stage it is important to allow time for the gymnasts to consolidate the newly learnt part otherwise the progression may not be successful. This method of coaching also allows the part skill to be revisited if the understanding or progression breaks down.

Many of the progressions or part skills can be practised on training aids such as floor-level apparatus, padded equipment or trampolines. The coach may also provide physical support to direct the shape of the movement and avoid the risk of injury at the various stages of development.

Typical Training Regimes

Every coach, regardless of the level at which they coach, has a duty of care towards the gymnasts they are coaching. The coach must therefore ensure that unnecessary risks are avoided, safe practices are used and that a safe environment is provided at all times.

It is generally recognized that it takes eight years to train a female gymnast to international standard, and around twelve years for a male gymnast. Consequently there should be no rush to accelerate the training, which might lead to over-training, overuse injury and possible burnout.

Designing the Training Regime

The main factors a coach should consider when designing the training programme to suit the individual needs of each gymnast include:

- The level of ability and aspirations of the child when determining the appropriate level of participation. The range of opportunities include fundamental movement and basic gymnastics, recreational non-competitive gymnastics, competitive gymnastics or high-performance gymnastics.
- The age and stage of maturation of the individual child. This is particularly important during periods of growth spurts in adolescents, where the growth in bone length exceeds the rate of development of the muscles and tendons. This has the effect of reducing the range of movement in the joints and co-ordination, making it harder to perform or learn skills.
- The type and level of skill appropriate to the age and stage of development of the gymnast. Some skills are best learnt

at particular stages in the child's development. If they are not mastered at the appropriate stage it may affect the long-term success of the gymnast's overall development.
- The appropriate level of training demand that will ensure suitable progress is made without the risk of overloading the gymnast either physically or psychologically.

To avoid the risk of the over-zealous coach or parent exploiting the precocious and talented young gymnast, great care must be taken when planning the training programme. If the training is excessive or overly demanding there is a risk of early burnout, where the young gymnast may not reach their full potential and is prematurely lost from the sport. Children of the same age develop at different rates both physically and psychologically, so there is a need for clear, constructive guidance on the duration and content of the age and stage of maturation-related training regimes. A number of countries where gymnastics was quite advanced had recognized the need to design the training programmes around the factors described above. However, the principles behind the design of the training plans were researched by Istvan Bayli and he devised a 'long-term athlete development' plan (LTAD), which is now adopted by many of the more forward-thinking governing bodies for sport. The plan is adapted to suit the individual sports, according to whether the sport is considered to be an early specializing or late specializing sport. Children usually begin specific training for gymnastics at an early age, at around six to eight years of age, so gymnastics is considered to be an early specializing activity. A typical customized gymnastics LTAD plan is described below.

The Long-Term Gymnast Development Plan

The development plan covers six stages of development and describes the recommended content and duration of the training programme.

Stage 1: Fundamentals (approximately ages five to eight) The programme should commence with the development of fundamental movement skills through a fun, enjoyable and suitably challenging environment. Progression is towards the introduction of fundamental gymnastic skills, including the acquisition of body shapes and body management. Participants in the fundamentals programme will normally train between 1 and 4 hours per week with sessions lasting between 45 minutes and 2 hours, depending upon the age and stage of development.

Stage 2: Learning to Train (approximately ages seven to nine) Gymnastics is considered to be an early specialization sport and children opting to enter into competitive gymnastics will begin to follow a specialist programme. This area of basic specialization will involve multi-lateral physical preparation and the acquisition of basic skills or elements leading to low-level competitions (four to six per year). A good work ethic and appropriate attitude may also be formed at this stage of development. Training between 10 and 12 hours per week is normal at this stage.

Stage 3: Training to Train (approximately ages ten to thirteen) Training up to 15 hours per week is normal, and the emphasis is on specialized physical preparation, learning and perfection of more advanced core skills and competing in intermediate age group events (six to eight per year).

Stage 4: Training to Compete (approximately ages fourteen to fifteen) The focus now is on specific physical preparation, the learning of more advanced core skills and participation in junior level competitions (eight to ten per year). Training hours are up to 20 hours per week at this stage.

Stage 5: Training to Win (approximately age sixteen-plus) The emphasis is on advanced physical preparation and the learning of high-performance skills and routines in order to compete in higher-level events (ten to fifteen per year). Training between 25 and 30 hours per week is required to reach the highest levels of attainment.

Stage 6: Retainment (senior and mature gymnasts) Having achieved high levels of performance, the gymnast maintains their level of physical fitness, refines the skills already learnt and consolidates their performance in high-level events. Training hours will be in the region of 25 hours per week.

In the later stages of their competitive careers many mature gymnasts reduce the training load by electing to train and compete on their better apparatus only. The choice of apparatus may be influenced by a higher level of success on the apparatus, a preference for that event or the onset of an injury that may prohibit training on other pieces of apparatus. In this way the gymnast can prolong their competitive career and may still compete for their country in the major events.

Planning the Training Programme

The factors described in the long-term gymnastic development plan are then translated into the individual gymnast's training programme.

If a gymnast is to achieve an optimal level of performance in competition, they must work to a meticulously planned training and event programme that is specifically designed to meet their individual needs. A long-term event programme may be designed for a four-year period, and quadrennial and long-term goals (targets) are set for this period. This long-term programme can then be broken down into an annual programme called the 'macro cycle', then further subdivided into various phases of training called 'meso cycles'. These phases of training are then reduced to weekly programmes, the 'micro cycles', where the fluctuating training load is identified. Finally, the programme is then translated into the gymnast's daily training diary, which sets out the training loads and targets for each session.

A useful and typical approach to designing and implementing the annual training and event programme is:

- Assess the gymnast's abilities, desires and training needs
- Set suitable long-term, medium-term and short-term event goals or targets
- Lay out the competition or event calendar for the four-year period
- Plan the annual programme, commencing with the competition period/s, then adding the various other phases of training in logical order
- Design the training schedule and content for each phase of training
- Devise the weekly and daily schedules
- Implement and continually monitor the plan
- Evaluate the information gathered through the monitoring process
- Review and modify the programme if the evaluation indicates a need for change.

The coach can then build the next programme on the outcomes and experience gained from the previous one.

The Annual Macro Cycle

The annual programme is usually divided into a number of cycles (meso cycles), each with specific phases of training, and there may be one, two or perhaps three cycles in one year. Typical meso cycles are:

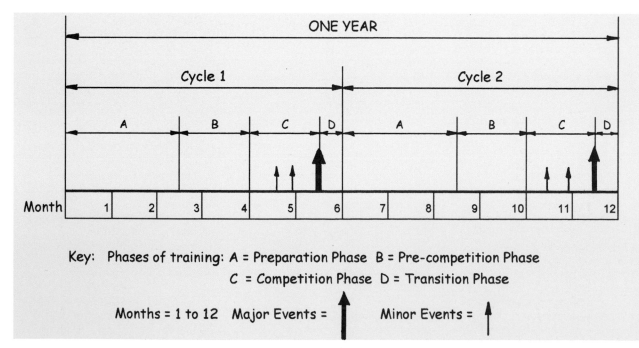

Typical two-cycle annual training and event programme.

WEEK PLAN   Training schedule: Competition Phase

Gymnast's name: Dates:

Day	Load	Warm Up	Pysical Prep.	Vault	A.Bars	Beam	Floor	Physical Prep.	Cool Down
Monday	Medium	30 min.	Choreo.	FX x 8	FX x 4	FX x 4	FX x 2	Endurance Strength	20 min.
Tuesday	Light	20 min.	General Strength		1/2 x 4	1/2 x 4	FX x 2	Flexibility	20 min.
Wednesday	Heavy	30 min		FX x 8	FX x 5	FX x 5	FX x 3		30 min.
Thursday	Light	20 min.	Choreo.		Single Skills	Single Skills	Single Skills	Specific Strength	20 min.
Friday	Rest	Rest	Rest	Rest	Rest	Rest	Rest	Rest	Rest
Saturday	Heavy	30 min.		FX x 8	FX x 5	FX x 5	FX x 3		30 mim.
Sunday	Light	20 min.	Specific Strength	FX x 4	FX x 1	FX x 1	FX x 1	Power Strength	20 min.

Key: FX = Full Exercise   1/2 = Half full exercise   x2 = repeat twice

Choreo. = Choreography   Single Skills = perfection of individual skills or dismounts

An example of a weekly plan for a female gymnast during the competition phase.

- **Preparation phase** (typically 70 per cent physical preparation and 30 per cent technical training) The concentration is on general physical preparation, endurance training, consolidation of core skills and learning individual skills and combinations of skills.
- **Pre-competition phase** (40 per cent physical preparation and 60 per cent technical training) The content includes general and specific physical preparation, perfection of skills and combinations and practising part and full routines.
- **Competition phase** (30 per cent physical preparation and 70 per cent technical training) The normally high work load is reduced in this phase to enable the gymnast to focus on specific physical preparation, consistency and quality of routines and mental preparation for the competitions.
- **Transition phase** After the demands of the competition phase a period of relaxation and recovery is implemented, followed by an introduction to the next cycle of training. This may include trying out new skills and consolidating previously learnt core skills.

Planning the Training Load

Gymnasts may regularly train up to 30 hours in one week and great care must be taken to ensure that they do not become fatigued through excessive loading. The coach must carefully plan the daily training load to ensure that the demands of training are sufficient to improve performance but also allow enough time for rest and recovery to take place. The daily workload will therefore be varied and will include heavy, medium and lightly loaded sessions together with rest periods. An example of a typical weekly plan for a competition phase is shown on p.27.

Structure of a Training Session

The gymnastic training session will usually be structured as follows:
1. Welcome the gymnasts and ascertain the state of their well-being
2. Outline the purpose of the session and focus attention on the session goals
3. Warm up for at least 20 minutes, including controlled stretching and foundation skills
4. Strength training or choreography
5. The main technical training part of the session
6. Strength training or flexibility training
7. Cool down
8. Period of self-reflection by the gymnasts and the coach
9. Summary appraisal of the session, feedback and focus for the next session.

The Warm-Up Session

The purpose of the warm-up is to raise the body temperature, improve blood circulation and increase the rate of breathing. This will then lead to the muscles becoming more flexible and more efficient and the increased blood flow will increase the energy available to the muscles. There will be less risk of injury to muscles and tendons and the gymnasts should also be more mentally prepared for the gymnastic training to follow.

Coaches vary the content and presentation of the warm-up to make it interesting and enjoyable. The initial content should comprise low-intensity exercises, such as team games, shuttle runs and relays or exercises to music to gradually increase the body temperature. The degree of activity should progressively increase through controlled stretching and mobility exercises to core or basic gymnastic skills.

The Cool-Down Session

A series of light exercises should be used to begin the recovery process and to facilitate the removal of waste products such as lactic acid from the muscles.

PART 3

THE PHYSICAL
PREPARATION
PROGRAMME

An artistic gymnast requires extraordinary levels of physical fitness and strength to train and compete at the highest levels. In Part 2 the importance of physical preparation was explained and examples given of the field tests that are used to measure the level of fitness. Each of the components of physical preparation, flexibility, strength and endurance can be improved by training methods specific to that component. In this section the methods and exercises used to develop the required physical profile will be explained and illustrated.

Flexibility Training

It is very important that the hyper-flexibility required in gymnastics is developed in young children between the ages of six and twelve before the body approaches the greatest period of growth and development. There are some very important physiological principles that underpin the methods used to develop the range of movement in the various joint complexes. However, for the purposes of this book, these principles have been incorporated into the following guidelines for flexibility training:

- Always warm up the whole body before flexibility training.
- The exercises must be slow and progressive over time.
- Ensure the correct alignment or position of the body part being stretched.
- Ensure that both sides of the body are equally stretched (front/back/left/right).
- Use a range of methods (such as those described later).
- The exercises may elicit slight feelings of burning or discomfort, but must not be painful.
- Specific flexibility training should be included in the training programme as a separate session or after the main aspects of the training session.

Following the hyper-stretching of a muscle it will temporarily lose up to 20 per cent of its contractile force, and this will adversely affect the power it could produce when attempting to perform dynamic skills. This is why flexibility training comes after, rather than before, the main technical part of the session, or as a separate session dedicated to improving the range of movement.

Methods Used to Develop Flexibility

When attempting to improve the range of movement in a joint complex we are trying to stretch the muscle fibres, connective tissue around the joint and the tendons that attach the muscles to the bones. Muscles work in pairs to move a limb. The contracting muscle, called the agonist, shortens to move the limb whilst the opposite muscle, the antagonist, relaxes. When attempting to improve the range of movement the muscle being targeted for the stretch is the antagonist, since we need this muscle to relax for the stretch to be effective. If we contract the agonist muscle the antagonist muscle will tend to relax proportionally.

Another key factor to note is that if we stretch a muscle quickly, sensory devices within the muscle sense the rate of stretch and this will invoke a response, which will try to shorten the muscle to protect it. The level of response will be proportional to the rate of the stretch of the muscle. A rapid or dynamic stretch will create a greater reflex response. This is known as the 'stretch reflex' or 'myotatic reflex' and will inhibit the effect of the stretch. Consequently the training methods used normally include slow, progressive stretches and prolonged holding of the final position.

Ballistic Stretching
This involves swinging the limb towards its full range of movement, for example leg swings. This tends to invoke a strong stretch reflex, which defeats the object of the exercise. This method is therefore not recommended if the main aim is to improve the range of movement. However, dynamic exercises are very useful as warm-up exercises and will help to improve the strength in the agonist (active) muscle, which is elevating or swinging the limb.

Passive Stretching
The gymnast relaxes the targeted muscle whilst an appropriate external force is applied to slowly stretch the muscle. The final position is held for between 20 and 60 seconds to allow the sensory devices to relax in order to reduce the resistance to the stretch. The prolonged hold of the final position will also allow the tendons to be stretched. The force of gravity, a suitable applied weight or a partner can provide the external force.

Active Stretching
In this method the gymnast actively contracts the agonist muscle to move the limb into the extended position. This causes the antagonist muscle to relax proportionally to the degree of contractile force in the agonist muscle and places the targeted muscle under stretch. The final position is normally held for 6 seconds and the exercise is repeated three times. This technique will also strengthen the agonist muscles and will enable the gymnast to lift the limb through the full range of movement.

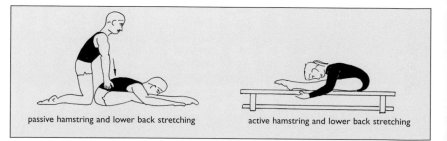

passive hamstring and lower back stretching   active hamstring and lower back stretching

Examples of passive and active stretching exercises.

Koko Tsurumi shows good active range during a split leap on the beam.

Proprioceptive Neuromuscular Facilitation (PNF) Stretching

If a muscle is contracted with a strong force and then the contraction is slowly removed, there will be an instant relaxation in the muscle. During this short period of relaxation the sensory devices within the muscle are also relaxed and the muscle can be slightly and slowly extended before the stretch reflex is evoked. This is the principle upon which PNF stretching methods are based.

There are two techniques used in the very effective PNF stretching process, both carried out with a partner.

Passive PNF Stretching

1. The partner raises the limb passively towards the full range of movement.
2. The partner fixes the position of the limb and the gymnast tries to press the limb downwards. This produces a strong 'isometric' contraction of the targeted muscles and is maintained for 6 seconds.
3. Upon slow relaxation of the isometric contraction the muscle sensory nerves momentarily relax and the partner is able to lift the limb to a slightly higher position to further stretch the targeted muscle.
4. The partner holds the new position of the limb and the gymnast produces another 6-second isometric contraction of the targeted muscle. Upon relaxation of the contraction the limb is lifted to a higher position.
5. The cycle is repeated three times on each limb.

Active PNF Stretching The principles used in this method of stretching are similar to those used in passive PNF stretching, but in this method the gymnast actively lifts the limb into its new raised position by contracting the agonist muscle.

1. The gymnast actively lifts the limb to its full range of movement by contracting the agonist muscle.
2. The partner then fixes the position of the limb and the gymnast tries to press the limb downwards to produce a strong isometric contraction of the target muscle. This is held for 6 seconds.

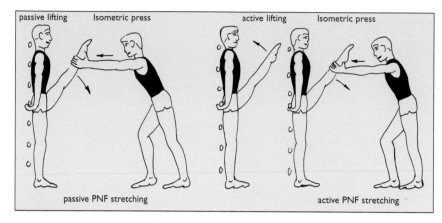

passive lifting   Isometric press   active lifting   Isometric press

passive PNF stretching   active PNF stretching

Examples of active and passive PNF stretching exercises.

STRENGTH TRAINING – KEY POINTS

- Care should be taken not to excessively overload the gymnast as this may lead to injury.
- Sufficient time must be allocated for rest and recovery between bouts of exercise.
- Good posture and correct technique must be used for best effect.
- The load demands must reflect the age and stage of maturation of each gymnast.
- Overtraining or excessive overloading may lead to poor performance in training, fatigue, repeated injuries, lethargy and lack of determination.

3. The isometric contraction is replaced by a contraction of the agonist muscle, causing the targeted antagonist muscle to relax.
4. The gymnast raises the limb to a slightly higher position followed by a further isometric contraction against the partner, who fixes the limb in the new position.
5. The sequence is repeated three times on each limb.

This method of stretching may not be as effective in improving the range of movement as the passive PNF technique but it has the added advantage of improving the strength of the agonist muscle. Both methods should be used to gain the greatest benefit. Together they will enable full expression of range of movement in active range elements such as split leaps, aerial walkovers, Thomas flairs and arabesques.

Typical Gymnastic Stretching Exercises

The methods of stretching described above can be applied to the many typical stretching exercises, some of which are illustrated opposite.

Strength Training

Strength training involves work on a range of different aspects, which include:

- **Maximum strength** The largest force produced by the contraction of the muscle fibres against an insurmountable load or resistance, for example a single maximum bench press
- **Concentric strength** The load that can be moved against gravity through the shortening of the muscle, for example the flexion of the elbow joint in a biceps curl
- **Eccentric strength** The load that can be lowered against the force of gravity during the extension of the muscle, for example the extension of the elbow in the biceps curl
- **Isometric strength** The force exerted in the muscle so that the force of contraction equals that of the load, for example a static held position such as a cross or planche
- **Power and speed** The ability of the neuromuscular systems to overcome a resistance with great speed of contraction of the muscle, for example a rapid muscular contraction in a dynamic gymnastic movement
- **Strength endurance** The ability to sustain a contraction of the muscle over a high number of repetitions.

Each of these forms of strength must be trained purposely through specific exercises and particular load demands.

Strength training programmes are based upon the principle that the human body will 'Specifically Adapt to Imposed Demands' – the SAID principle. This requires that we progressively overload the body in order that it will adapt and become stronger.

This 'overloading' involves exercising the muscles to a percentage of their maximum load over a number of repetitions and then progressively increasing the load or demand over time as the muscles become stronger.

Training for Maximum Strength

The maximum force a muscle or group of muscles can exert in one contraction is called the maximum strength. This is trained by performing a small number of repetitions (five to seven) with near maximum load (80–90 per cent of the maximum load) and carrying out three sets of the exercise. The load can be increased as the muscles become stronger.

Training for Power Strength

Powerful muscular contractions are needed to produce the fast, dynamic movements of gymnastic skills. Power is trained by performing between six and ten fast repetitions of the exercise with medium load (50–80 per cent of

shoulder stretching

hamstring and lower back stretching

front splits stretching

hips and straddle fold stretching

Some typical gymnastic stretching exercises.

maximum load), and repeating this in three sets with rest intervals of around 3 minutes between each set.

Another very effective training method for the development of power is plyometric training. This involves the pre-stretching of the muscle prior to the explosive contraction of the muscle. This enables the muscle to contract with up to 30 per cent more force to create the powerful movement. Typical plyometric exercises include spring jumping on one or two legs, hopping on one leg or depth jumping. The exercise and load demand must be carefully selected to suit the stage of development of the individual gymnast. Plyometric depth jumping exercises should not be used with pre-pubescent children, since the impact loads will be too great for their developing bodies.

Training for Isometric Strength

Static or held parts are gymnastic features that require isometric muscular contractions in order to hold a body position. This involves producing strong muscular forces without a shortening of the muscle. The method used to develop isometric strength is to carry out five to ten repetitions of maximum isometric exertion held for 5–7 seconds. Three sessions per week are recommended, with sufficient time for recovery allowed between sessions. This type of training is very specific to the body position and it is important that the correct final position is maintained. A typical example is the cross on rings.

The gymnast needs to be able to lower or lift into or out of the static position.

ABOVE: The plyometric training exercise known as depth jumping.

RIGHT: Maxim Devyatovskiy from Russia holding a cross on the rings.

This requires a degree of eccentric strength to lower into the position and concentric strength to lift or press out of the position. The training for static held parts usually includes repetition of the eccentric lowering into and concentric pressing out of the skill in conjunction with the static position being held. A typical programme for the development of the strength required to perform a cross on rings is described later in the book.

Training for Local Muscular Endurance

Gymnastic skills are learnt through the performance of many repetitions of the skill. The gymnast must therefore be able to perform the skill repeatedly before fatigue sets in, which requires a high level of local muscular endurance. This may be acquired by performing up to five sets of twenty or more repetitions of an exercise with a light load of around 20–50 per cent of maximum load. Rest intervals of between 30 and 60 seconds are incorporated between bouts of exercise. This method of local muscular endurance training is called interval training.

Another method is to perform a series of light exercises at different exercise stations, for periods of 30 seconds interspaced with rest intervals of 30 seconds. In this form of circuit training, the type of exercise and number of repetitions can be varied to make the training more interesting. As the gymnasts become fitter the rest intervals between each exercise station can be reduced and the number of repetitions at each station increased.

Designing a Strength Training Programme

Many of the exercises used in a gymnastic strength training programme will closely simulate the gymnastic skills to ensure that maximum benefits are gained. Some typical exercises have been illustrated in this chapter, and a selection of these can be used to construct a programme to suit the age and stage of maturation of each gymnast. The number of repetitions and the degree of difficulty (loading) can be varied to make the exercises appropriate for maximum strength, power or speed

strength, endurance and so on. It is advisable to alternate the targeted group of muscles in each successive set of exercises to allow some recovery of the stored muscle energy, and it is important that both sides of the body are equally catered for. It is also recommended that the strength training should not cease more than five days before an event or strength may begin to deteriorate.

Endurance Training

Training for Aerobic Fitness

Most gymnastic exercises require short bursts of muscular activity and utilize the energy stored in the muscles. This is known as anaerobic exercise (without oxygen). To perform sequences of many repetitions of a skill or practice routines the gymnast must however have good aerobic (with oxygen) fitness. This often overlooked type of fitness can be trained by alternating between sessions of:

- **Interval training** A light exercise is carried out twenty to thirty times in one set followed by a rest for 30–60 seconds. The sequence is then repeated up to five times. The length of the rest interval or duration of exercise can be varied according to the level of fitness.
- **Circuit training** A circuit of exercise stations is constructed and the exercise at each station is performed a prescribed number of times (or for a set duration of time) before moving on to the next station.
- **Jogging** up to 3km.
- **Back-to-back routines** The cardiovascular and aerobic fitness levels can be improved by performing back to back slightly reduced content gymnastic routines, without rest in between.

A high level of aerobic fitness must be achieved before the gymnast approaches the pre-competition phase to enable them to practise the half and full routines safely. The phase of training in which the gymnasts repeatedly perform competition exercises will also enhance the level of cardiovascular and aerobic fitness.

hip flexor muscles

mid-body core stability exercises

Typical gymnastic strength training exercises for various parts of the body.

Supplementary Fitness Training

Most high-performance training programmes will include dance and choreography as an integral part of the training. This will contribute to the posture, strength, style and techniques used throughout the gymnastic programme.

More mature gymnasts sometimes train with free weights to create specific concentrated loads. However, the majority of the strength and fitness training exercises used in gymnastics rely on the gymnast's own body weight as the resistance. Weight pads such as ankle, wrist or waist belts can be used to supplement the loading of the exercise.

upper body: pushing exercises

pulling exercises

static strength exercises

leg strengthening exercises

Typical gymnastic strength training exercises for various parts of the body (continued).

PART 4

TECHNICAL SKILLS IN WOMEN'S GYMNASTICS

The specific competition requirements for each apparatus were described in Part 3 under Rules and Regulations. This section will provide an insight into the techniques used to perform a selection of skills and how they may be learnt. There are many gymnastic elements and it would be an enormous task to describe them all. For the purposes of this book, a selection of important foundation or core skills and some more advanced elements are illustrated. This book is not intended to be a definitive training manual, and advice should be sought from a qualified gymnastics coach before attempting any of the skills or techniques described.

Vault

Vaulting is a very dynamic activity and in a competition the vault, including the run-up, will be completed in just a few seconds. The gymnasts and their coach will select the type of vaults the gymnast will perform on the basis of the gymnast's power, arm and shoulder propulsion strength, the ability to rotate forwards or backwards and the propensity to twist around the long axis of the body. The more complex vaults involve multiple somersaults combined with a number of twists, and these require a high level of spatial awareness as well as good technique.

In recreational gymnastics or novice events the participants will learn and perform vaults such as the squat through vault and straddle vault. These provide the novice gymnasts the opportunity to experience the fundamental concepts of vaulting without having to perform the more difficult vaults.

The Handspring Vault

The handspring vault is perhaps the most important basic vault in both men's and women's gymnastics since it successfully introduces all the key concepts of vaulting.

KEY CONCEPTS IN VAULTING

There is a wide family of vaults but there are some key concepts which are common to all vaults:
- A dynamic but controlled run-up
- A fast and low pre-jump onto the springboard
- Powerful take-off from the springboard
- Flight onto the vaulting table
- Repulsion through the arms from the table
- Trajectory from the table with desired flight path and degree of rotation
- Changes of body shape or position during the flight phase as required by the particular vault
- A controlled landing.

HANDSPRING VAULT – KEY POINTS

- The run-up should be controlled but dynamic.
- The jump onto the springboard should be low, with the arms circling backwards.
- The feet should arrive on the board in front of the hips with the arms behind the body. The body is slightly 'dished'.
- There should be a powerful thrust from the legs against the board as the arms are swung forwards and upwards into the take-off.
- In the flight onto the platform, lift the heels strongly and reach quickly with the arms to contact the vault table. The body is slightly arched or straight.
- The body will pivot around the hands. The thrust through the arms and shoulders must occur just before the handstand position. The head is held backwards.
- The body remains stretched to slightly arched during the flight phase and the degree of rotation is controlled by moving the arms upwards or to the side.
- The body is slightly dished and the arms move forwards and sideways to control the rotation in readiness for the landing. The head tilts slightly forwards.
- The feet arrive in front of the body and a force is applied through the legs and feet against the landing surface to arrest the rotation and forward momentum of the body.
- The arms press downwards and the legs, hips and ankles bend to control the landing.

It also forms the basis for a number of the more advanced vaults.

Before the handspring vault can be effectively learnt the gymnast must be able to demonstrate that she can hold good mid-body tension in a straight body handstand, take off efficiently from the springboard and land safely and well.

The coach will ensure that the gymnast is adequately prepared physically and will use a number of progressive skills or drills to develop the full vault. Some of these useful part skills are shown later.

The coach will seek to prevent or eradicate the common execution faults such as bending of the arms and legs, dropping the head forwards, loose body and moving the shoulders in front of the hands whilst in contact with the platform. The use of progressive part-skills or drills will help to ensure that each stage of the vault is correctly learnt and consistently performed. This will minimize the possibility of the faults occurring.

Handspring with Twist

Once the handspring vault has been mastered, it is possible to raise the difficulty of the vault by adding one or more twists in the flight phase of the vault. The illustration shows a single or full twist but often up to two and a half twists are included by the more skilful gymnasts.

The handspring vault technique.

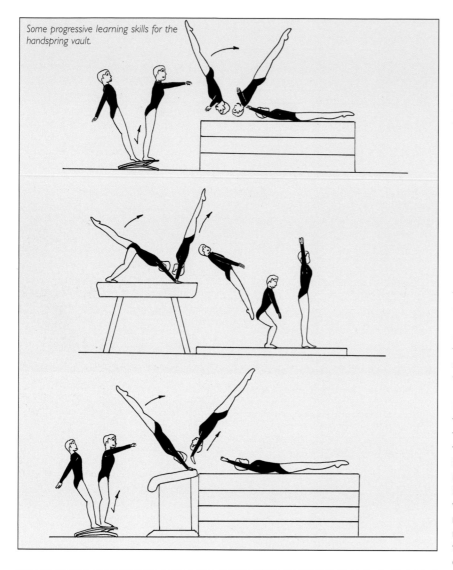

Some progressive learning skills for the handspring vault.

The handspring vault with an added twist.

Before the twist can be introduced the gymnast must be able to consistently perform the handspring vault with a high controlled flight from the platform. This requires good arm and shoulder strength together with accurate timing to propel the gymnast from the platform prior to the vertical position. The body should be straight to facilitate the twist around the long axis of the body.

It is very important for the gymnast and coach to establish the natural or preferred direction of twist prior to including a twist in any skill. The easiest way to do this is to ask the gymnast to perform a jump with half turn, a fall backwards to front support on a safety mat and a fall forwards to back lie on a safety mat. Hopefully the direction of turn will be the same in each activity. If the left shoulder moves in a backwards direction this is classified as a 'twist to the left' and vice versa. It is imperative that once the natural or preferred direction of twist has been established this direction should prevail when learning any skill which involves a twist.

The twist should occur after the hands have left the platform. The most effective technique for creating the twist is to use the aerial tilt twist method. To create a twist to the left as shown in the illustration, the gymnast must press the right arm sideways and downwards at the instant the hands leave the platform. This will cause the body to tilt off axis, and the right side of the body, having less resistance to rotation, will accelerate forwards around the raised left arm. The degree of twist will be controlled by how vigorously the arm action is made. The aim is to complete the twist before the apex of the flight path is reached. Once the required twist has been completed the right arm is raised sideways and upwards to remove the tilt and arrest the twist. The arms are then used to control the degree of somersault rotation in readiness for the landing.

It is possible to create the twist by producing a torque through the hands against the platform. The problem with this type of twist is that it can not be arrested until the feet contact the landing surface, enabling an opposite torque to be applied through the feet to stop the twist. This greatly complicates the landing and is more difficult to control. Therefore the torque twist technique is not advocated.

The coach will teach the twisting vault through various progressive stages and these will often include those listed below.

Typical Progressions

1. Handspring to land on the back on a pile of safety mats at platform height
2. Handspring with half and full twist to flat body landing on safety mats
3. Handspring with half and full twist over the platform to land in a landing pit
4. As above but to land on safety mats in the landing pit, the height of mats being gradually increased until level with the floor
5. As above but to land on a safety mat on the landing module
6. Full vault to land on the competition landing pad.

The coach may assist by supporting the gymnast at the take-off at the point of propulsion from the horse or by spotting the landing.

Yurchenko Vault with Twist

The Yurchenko vault is named after the Soviet gymnast Natalia Yurchenko, who was the first gymnast to perform the vault, and is a popular vault in both men's and women's artistic gymnastics. It requires the gymnast to perform a round-off onto the springboard followed by a backward take-off into backward handspring onto the platform. A stretched backward somersault is then introduced in the flight from the hands.

Before learning the Yurchenko vault, the gymnast must be able to repeatedly and consistently perform a powerful round-off, a back flip and a stretched back somersault.

The coach will use a number of progressive skills to teach the basic Yurchenko vault and a typical preparation, as well as the actual vault, is shown later.

In the early stages of learning some common errors may crop up and the coach will try to prevent or correct these errors at each stage. Such errors might include misalignment after the round-off; bending too deeply at the knees on the board; throwing the head backwards on the take-off; being too high in the flight on to the platform; bending the knees during the snap action; and piking the legs downwards from the handstand position.

Once the basic vault has been learnt, one or more twists can be added to the somersault phase. This vault is actually a stretched backward somersault from the hands with a full twist around the long axis

Anna Myzdrikova of Russia performing a Yurchenko vault.

Progressive learning drills for the Yurchenko vault and the Yurchenko full twist.

of the body. The twist is introduced as an aerial twist action after the hands have left the vaulting table. To create a twist to the left the right arm is momentarily raised as the left arm is forced downwards to the left hip. This tilts the body and initiates the twist. The right arm is then pulled downwards across the chest to accelerate the twist. The arms are raised and opened upon completion of the twist to remove the twist and to control the somersault rotation in readiness for the landing.

YURCHENKO VAULT – KEY POINTS

- The run-up must be carefully controlled and slower than for most other vaults.
- Take care to achieve the correct alignment in the round-off.
- The arm thrust from the floor and the 'snap-up' action must rotate the body and lift the chest and shoulders upwards and backwards.
- The feet should arrive on the board behind the hips, the body should be dished and the arms held just below shoulder height.
- The drive through the legs should lift the hips forwards and upwards.
- As the legs leave the board the shoulders should be just behind the hips with arms driving upwards and backwards.
- The head should move in unison with the arms during the flight onto the platform.
- The hands should quickly reach backwards towards the platform and the hips and legs should be level with the height of the shoulders as the hands contact the platform.
- The body rotates around the shoulders and hands before the arm thrust and snap-up action are introduced through the handstand position.
- As the arms leave the platform the arms are driven towards the thighs, the shoulders lift upwards and backwards into the somersault.
- The body should be stretched or slightly dished during the flight.
- The arms are then used to control the rotation in readiness for the landing.
- The feet should make contact with the landing module just behind the hips to allow the somersault rotation to be arrested by pressing through the feet.

Asymmetric Bars

Many of the skills performed by the female gymnasts on the asymmetric bars are similar to those the men perform on horizontal bar but with the complication of the second bar.

The competitive routines on the asymmetric bars must include giant swings, close bar skills, release and re-catch elements, movements on both bars and transfers between the bars. The selection of moves described below will provide an insight into the type of skill frequently demonstrated on the bars by the female gymnasts.

Forward Giant Swing

The backward and forward giant swings are the basis of asymmetric bar routines. The forward giant is covered below and a description of the backward giant can be found in the section on the horizontal bar.

The forward giant swing performed by Veronica Wagner (Sweden).

FORWARD GIANT SWING –
KEY POINTS

- Grasp the bar in under-grasp with the heel of the hand leading the swing.
- From the front support position, cast into the handstand position.
- Fully extend the body before displacing the heels to commence the downswing.
- In the first quarter of the swing extend the body to maximize the swing potential.
- Draw the hips into a pike to allow the legs to clear the bottom bar.
- Accelerate the legs and heels under the bar into a slight body arch.
- On the upswing, press downwards on the bar, dish the body and close the shoulder angle. This allows the swing momentum to be retained on the upswing.
- Lead with the shoulders and hold a slight dished body shape into the handstand.
- Re-grasp with the hands and extend the body through the handstand position.

The gymnast must have excellent mid-body core stability in the handstand position and the ability to dynamically close and open the shoulder angle before attempting to learn the giant swing.

A useful series of preparatory drills for learning the forward giant might include:
- On a floor bar, fall from handstand to back lie on a safety mat.
- On a single polished bar with gloves and loops, cast to handstand and forward giant (for more information on the use of gloves and loops, see the section on the horizontal bar).
- On a single asymmetric bar practise the forward giant with physical support from the coach.
- As above but with a rope or elastic strand strung across the uprights to represent the lower bar.

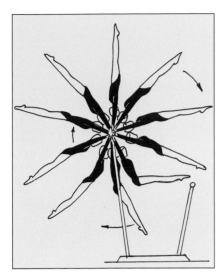

The technique for the forward giant swing.

The Endo circle on asymmetric bars.

GIENGER SALTO – KEY POINTS

- In the downswing a 'timing swing' is introduced – dish-arch-kick – to set up the required action.
- The body should be fully extended to slightly arched beneath the bar.
- On the upswing drive the legs and close the hip and shoulder angle slightly.
- As the centre of mass approaches the horizontal line through the bar the feet initiate the turn and the bar is released.
- During the flight phase, the body remains dished as the body continues to half twist and somersault. The legs must circle upwards and towards the bar before circling under the body and away from the bar.
- Sight the bar just before reaching to re-grasp it.
- Upon re-grasp press against the bar to extend the body into the downswing.

- Forward giant on the asymmetric bars with coach assistance until the skill is mastered.

Care must be taken to avoid the heels colliding with the lower bar or loss of grip, which is most likely to occur at the point of greatest momentum as the gymnast passes beneath the bar.

ENDO CIRCLE – KEY POINTS

- Cast into handstand in under-grasp.
- Commence the downswing fully extended then straddle the legs and close the hips into a straddle deep body fold, the Japana position. The shoulder angle is fully open to maximize the swing potential.
- Keep the thighs pressed into the chest on the downswing.
- Close the shoulder angle and hold the straddle pike position beneath the bar.
- On the upswing press down on the bar, holding the thighs into the chest.
- As the centre of mass and shoulders rise above the bar, rotate the hips over the shoulders into the Japana position above the bar.
- From this position above the bar the legs circle sideways through to straddle lift to handstand.

Endo Circle

The Endo circle may be described as a circle in straddled support in a forwards direction from handstand and returning into handstand. The very technical skill may be performed on the high or low bar. It requires good flexibility in the hips and shoulders and good technique in a straddle lift to handstand. The Endo circle is almost a mirror image of the Stalder circle, which rotates backwards around the bar.

To help the gymnast understand this skill the coach will almost certainly teach the forward roll into straddled support followed by a lift to handstand. Another very useful drill is to perform a cast from support into Japana support and Endo circle forwards to return to Japana support. This may be performed on a single polished bar with gloves and loops or on the chalk bar. This will ensure that the correct technique is understood before the element is attempted from the handstand position.

Gienger Salto

The Gienger salto is named after the German male gymnast Eberhard Gienger,

who was the first gymnast to perform this skill. It is now frequently performed by both male and female gymnasts. The Gienger salto may be described as a backward giant swing into a backward somersault with a half turn to re-catch the

Ida Jonson (Sweden) performing a Gienger salto on the bars.

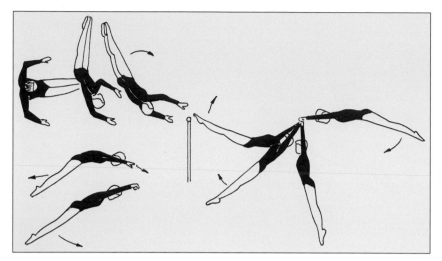

ABOVE: The technique for the Gienger salto.

RIGHT: Becky Downey (GB) during a transfer between the bars.

bar. It is classified as a release and re-catch element.

It is imperative that before attempting to learn the Gienger salto, the gymnast is familiar with the backward fly away from the bar. It may also be helpful if the gymnast was able to perform a stretched backward somersault with half turn to front body landing on a safety mat on the trampoline. This will improve the spatial awareness and understanding of the pattern of movement.

Perhaps the best way to learn this skill is on a single bar over a pitted landing area and with a padded bar. The gymnast can perform many attempts gradually bringing the somersault closer to the bar until it is possible to re-grasp the bar consistently. The gymnast may wear heel pads to protect the heels should they collide with the bar. The coach may also support the gymnasts, initially at the hips throughout the skill and then spotting the gymnast just prior to re-grasping the bar.

Only after many successful attempts in such a set-up should the skill be progressed to the normal landing area. A safety mat should be provided beneath the bar, and the coach should support the gymnast until the skill is perfected in this situation.

During a competition the coach is entitled to be present at the asymmetric bars to provide support to the gymnast if the re-grasp is not successful.

Transfer Between the Bars

The flighted element between the bars can be performed in a forwards or backwards direction, with or without a turn and may transfer from the low to high bar or vice versa. In all cases momentum in the initial circling action must be converted into a flight path that will allow the gymnast to rotate or turn to re-grasp the second bar. A successful performance will enable the gymnast to

maintain the swing upon re-catch and to progress with smooth transition into the next skill.

This type of element will invariably be taught over a pitted landing area or suitably matted area. During the early stages of learning the second bar will be removed and replaced by a rope or elastic strand to simulate the second bar. The gymnast may also land upon a carefully positioned pile of safety mats as an intermediate progression.

As the gymnast's confidence and awareness grows the second bar may be replaced, possibly with the pile of safety mats remaining in place, and the gymnast is able to re-grasp the bar but land safely on the mats. In the initial attempts at the full skill the coach will support the gymnast throughout the skill, then 'shadow and spot' until the skill is consolidated. The coach may also shadow and spot the gymnast during the competition to reduce the risk of injury in the event of a mishap.

Balance Beam

To perform skills on the beam the gymnast must possess great skill, balance, artistry and immense courage. The dance and linking skills will be developed during the choreography sessions and the gymnastic skills will be mastered on the floor before progressing through various stations onto the beam. The normal development of beam skills will follow the pattern described below.

1. Firstly learn and master the skills on the floor.
2. Perform the skill or combination of skills on a line drawn on the carpeted floor.
3. Practise on a strip of mat equal in width to the beam.
4. Progress to a low floor beam with surrounding mats.
5. Rehearse the skills on a progressively higher beam with safety mats level with the height of the beam placed on each side.
6. Transfer to the full-height beam with safety mats alongside. Often additional padding may be attached to the beam to soften the impact.
7. Perform on the high beam in connection with other skills.

The coach may provide physical support at each stage of the learning.

Split Leap

The split leap requires a high degree of active range of movement in the splits range together with leg strength to generate height and to control the landing.

SPLIT LEAP – KEY POINTS

- An excellent range of movement in the hips must be developed through flexibility training (see the section on passive flexibility training exercises for forward and sideways splits in Part 3).
- Active range of movement exercises such as active PNF flexibility training must be used to develop the active flexibility in the hips and legs.
- The repetition of split leaps on the trampoline will increase the active range and leg strength.
- The element is then progressed in the sequence described.

The photograph shows an excellent example of a forward split leap, with an imaginative body and arm position adding a unique style to the performance.

A fine example of a split leap performed by Yang Li of China.

Rebecca Bross (USA) performing a free walkover on the beam.

Free Walkover

This skill is very difficult since it requires the gymnast to perform an open-body, split-leg, forward somersault with momentary landing on one leg.

This element requires good technical skill and will undoubtedly be developed using the progressive sequence for learning beam skills as described earlier.

The technique for the free walkover.

FREE WALKOVER – KEY POINTS

- Step forward into a deep lunge with the chest close to the front thigh.
- Drive the arms downwards as the rear leg drives upwards.
- Power the arms backwards, upwards and sideways as the front leg is powerfully straightened to cause the elevation.
- Maintain the strong arched position with the head upwards.
- The foot of the lead leg must land under the centre of mass with the heel being lowered quickly onto the beam.
- The top leg is held high as the front body is pulled forwards and upright.
- The arms are used to control the balance.
- The second foot is rapidly placed on the beam for greater control.

Balance

The balance positions on the beam range from a classical position such as a handstand or single leg balance to very original shapes or leg positions that demonstrate great skill, strength and originality. Different body parts can be used as the base for the balance, as can be seen in the unique shoulder balance. Imaginative ways of entering into and moving out of the balance add interest and variety to the beam routines.

RIGHT: Ana Tamirjan (Romania) in an interesting balance on the beam.

FAR RIGHT: A distinctive pose by Anna Myzdrikova.

Artistic Expression

The movements that are used to link the beam elements together usually involve co-ordinated arm and body movements performed within traditional dance elements and leaps or jumps. The movements are choreographed to show artistic expression and to reflect the personal characteristics of each gymnast. Great effort and imagination goes into ensuring variety and originality in the movements.

Floor Exercise

A women's artistic competitive floor routine will include a variety of linked tumbles, leaps and jumps joined together with choreographed dance movements. The selection of skills shown below will give a good indication of frequently used core and advanced gymnastic floor skills.

Dance and Choreography

The dance and choreography will usually be designed to reflect the personality and character of the individual gymnast and should blend with the rhythm and tempo of the music. Classical ballet elements or national dance characteristics may also be intrinsic within the routines. Many hours practising gymnastic leaps combined with classic ballet barre and choreographic dance training will develop posture, strength and freedom of artistic expression. Once a repertoire of leaps, dance and ballet skills have been learnt, the choreographer, coach and gymnast can work together to design interesting and imaginative routines. It is very important that the gymnast enjoys performing the routine as this will inspire them to express themselves in the performance of the routine.

Back Flip

This gymnastic skill has a number of names and is often referred to as a 'flick flack' or 'backward handspring' as well as 'back flip'. For this book we will use the term back flip. The back flip is frequently preceded by a round-off to become a very important backward accelerator skill. This combination of skills must be accurately performed to provide a consistent and powerful entry into the take-off for backward somersaults. The back flip is usually taught from a static entry and the technique perfected before being added to the round-off.

Expressive choreography from Yamamoto of Japan.

When the back flip is linked to a round-off as an accelerator the final position of the feet in relation to the centre of mass at the exit from the back flip is critical. This will depend upon the type of skill that will follow the back flip:

• For a series of back flips the feet should be in front of the hips to create a low backwards trajectory.

An illustration of the back flip technique.

BACK FLIP – KEY POINTS

• Move off balance in a dished shape, with the centre of mass moving behind the feet and the arms moving forwards and downwards towards the thighs.
• Bend at the knees, keeping the feet flat to the floor and the knees behind the feet.
• The back muscles are used to drive the upper body backwards and the legs quickly straighten into a low backward trajectory.
• The arms drive quickly upwards and backwards but the head is held still.
• The hands contact the floor with the body arched after a low and long flight path.
• Snap the body into a dished shape through the handstand and thrust from the arms to drive up the shoulders.
• The body should rotate in a dished shape.
• The flight from the hands should be high and short, with the feet contacting the floor just in front of the centre of mass.
• The end position should be in a dished shape with the arms just below shoulder height in readiness for entry into another skill.

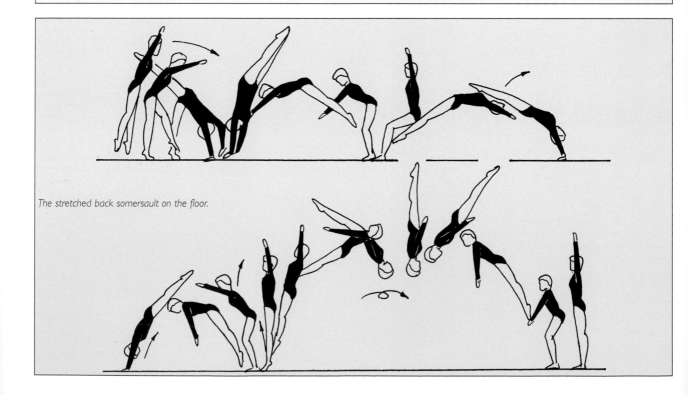

The stretched back somersault on the floor.

- For a tempo or whip back somersault the feet should be directly under the hips to generate an intermediate backwards flight path.
- For a high backward somersault the feet must be just behind the hips to force the hips upwards into a higher trajectory.

Stretched Back Somersault

The stretched back somersault is the foundation for most backward tumble skills and is normally preceded by a round-off back flip combination to generate the momentum for the somersault.

It may take considerable time for the young gymnast to develop the technique and power to consistently perform the round-off, back flip, stretched back somersault combination. However, this sequence of skills, if performed correctly,

forms the foundation for a wide range of more advanced backward somersault skills.

Once the stretched back somersault has been mastered twists can be added to increase the difficulty rating, or it can be used as the basis for learning the double back somersault.

Double Back Somersault

The double back somersault comprises two full rotations in one take-off and it can be performed in the tucked, piked or

even the stretched body shape. The double back somersault is usually preceded by the round-off back flip combination in order to generate the height of flight and rotation required to perform the double somersault. The photograph shows a double piked somersault being performed; this would be developed from the tucked version described below.

Beth Tweddle performing a double piked somersault.

STRETCHED BACK SOMERSAULT –
KEY POINTS

- The exit from the round-off back flip should be with the feet just behind the hips with the body in a dished shape and the arms at shoulder height.
- As the legs straighten the hips push forwards and upwards and the arms drive upwards. This creates the required powerful take-off action required to generate height and rotation for the somersault.
- The shoulders will be just behind the hips but the head should remain neutral.
- As the feet leave the floor the arms are dropped to the front or side to reduce the resistance to rotation and the body will rotate about the centre of mass.
- The body remains slightly arched through the inverted position to facilitate rotation.
- The body then dishes and the arms are lifted to control the rotation in readiness for the landing.
- The feet should arrive on the floor just behind the hips to help to stop the rotation.
- The hips, knees and ankles are flexed and the arms are pressed downwards to absorb the impact of landing.

Some development drills for the double back somersault. Each progression would be preceded by a round-off, back flip combination.

DOUBLE TUCKED BACK SOMERSAULT – KEY POINTS

- Sufficient momentum must be generated in the round-off, back flip.
- At the exit from the back flip the feet must be placed just behind the hips and the body should be in an open dished shape, arms around shoulder height.
- The legs are powerfully pushed straight, forcing the hips forwards and upwards whilst driving the arms upwards. This is the critical phase in the skill as the take-off must provide the appropriate trajectory, momentum and rotation.
- The extended body shape at the take-off will generate a large turning effect from the floor.
- Immediately the feet leave the floor the arms are driven downwards and thighs quickly lifted upwards into the tucked shape. This reduces the resistance to rotation and the somersault accelerates.
- As the tuck is initiated the head must remain neutral and must not be thrown backwards.
- The hands grasp the shins and pull the legs into a tight tuck and the shoulders are forced upwards and backwards into the somersault.
- The aim is to complete one and a half rotations before the top of the flight path is reached.
- As the gymnast enters the final third of the second somersault the legs and body are gradually extended and the arms are lifted to reduce the rotation in preparation for the landing.
- Upon landing the feet are placed behind the hips in order to stop the somersault rotation.
- The ankles, knees and hips are flexed under control and the arms are pressed downwards to absorb the impact of the landing.

PART 5

TECHNICAL SKILLS IN MEN'S GYMNASTICS

There are six pieces of apparatus in the men's artistic programme and the order of performance in a competition is: floor exercise; pommel horse (or side horse); still rings; vault; parallel bars; and horizontal bar. The competition requirements for each of the men's apparatus are described in Part 3, under Rules and Regulations. In this part a selection of basic foundation skills and some more advanced skills on each apparatus are described, together with typical key points. This section will also provide an insight into how the skills can be learnt and performed.

This book is not intended to be a definitive coaching manual and advice from an appropriately qualified gymnastics coach must be sought before attempting any of the skills described.

Floor Exercise

The competitive floor exercise routine will contain a variety of combined tumbles, somersaults with and without twists and will include elements of strength, flexibility and balance. A range of these elements are described to give a broad sample of the frequently performed floor skills.

Stretched Front Somersault

This skill is frequently used in modern gymnastics and is often performed in combination with handsprings or flysprings together with other somersaults, some with twists added to increase the difficulty value.

The position of the feet relative to the hips upon landing will vary according to the skill that may be linked to the somersault. In order to accommodate an entry into another stretched forward somersault the feet must be placed directly under or slightly behind the hips to allow a forward flight path with a high degree of rotation.

When learning the stretched front somersault the sequence of progressions may be as follows:
1. Run in to front somersault tucked to stand on the floor.
2. Front somersault tucked from a springboard to stand on a waist-high pile of safety mats.
3. Stretched three-quarter front somersault from a springboard to back lie on the pile of safety mats.
4. Stretched front somersault from a springboard to land on feet on a two-high pile of safety mats.
5. Run into a stretched front somersault to land on a safety mat or landing pad on the floor.

The coach may provide physical support to ensure the safety of the gymnast.

If the gymnast is fortunate enough to be training in a modern facility with a sunken floor-level trampoline adjacent to a landing pit and possibly a sprung tumbling track, then the learning programme can be enhanced. The stretched front somersault can be practised on the trampoline or from the trampoline onto safety mats placed in the landing pit. Consecutive front somersaults can be practised on and from the trampoline, landing on the safety mats.

Combination tumbles comprising handspring or flysprings into consecutive front somersaults can be gradually built up on the sprung tumble track with less impact on the body.

Once the stretched front somersault has been perfected a twist can be included to add variety and increase the difficulty value. The more advanced gymnasts may demonstrate combinations of backwards and forwards somersaults with and without a half or more twists.

STRETCHED FRONT SOMERSAULT – KEY POINTS

- The momentum to perform the stretched front somersault may be generated from a short run or from an accelerated handspring or flyspring.
- Arrive with the feet just ahead of the centre of mass with the body slightly arched and the arms overhead.
- Drive the arms forward at shoulder height and move the shoulders forwards to dish the body.
- Push downwards and forwards through the feet to set up the take-off and create the large turning effect against the floor.
- The flight path must be forwards with a little elevation to permit the fast rotation.
- As the feet leave the floor drive the heels upwards to arch the body and force the arms sideways at shoulder height. This will reduce the resistance to rotation and cause the somersault speed to increase.
- The shoulders will drop as the body rotates around the centre of mass but the head should remain slightly upwards until the last half of the somersault.
- The head should then tilt forwards as the feet descend towards the floor.
- The position of the arms will be used to control the degree of rotation just prior to landing and the feet must be placed just in front or under the centre of mass.
- The ankles, knees and hips will flex to absorb the landing.

Forward Splits

Jumps and leaps are not so prolific in men's artistic gymnastics as in women's, and it is more usual for the men to demonstrate their range of movement by performing some splits-type element.

See the section on Flexibility Training in Part 3 for the training methods gymnasts use to improve their range of movement in the hips in order to successfully perform the splits. The judges will be looking for the legs to be flat to the floor with the rear heel directly on top of the rear foot and pointing upwards.

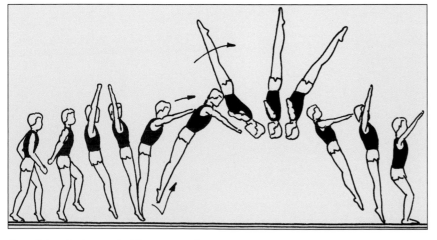
The technique for the stretched front somersault.

Kohei Uchimura performs the forward splits on the floor.

This indicates that the hips are correctly aligned and that the splits are accurately performed.

THOMAS FLAIRS – KEY POINTS

- The gymnast must have good range of movement in the side and front splits, and excellent active range of movement in the hips and legs.
- A high degree of upper body strength is also imperative.
- The gymnast must pass through a high straddled front support position before lifting the lead leg upwards, allowing the lower leg to circle forwards into a splits position.
- From the back support position the lower leg is lifted towards the shoulder into splits to allow the other leg to circle rearwards towards the top planche position in front support.
- The sequence of actions is then repeated to form the complete flair.
- The gymnast must maintain a high support position, with the hips extended in the front and particularly the back support position.

Mathias Fahig (Germany) shows good amplitude in the Thomas flairs.

The Thomas flair technique.

Thomas Flairs

A number of pommel horse skills are used in the men's floor exercises and they can attract quite high difficulty values since they require good technique and amplitude when performed on the floor. One example of a recognized pommel horse element being used to good effect on the floor is the Thomas flair. This element was first performed on the pommel horse by the US gymnast Kurt Thomas. The skill may be best explained as a pommel circle performed with the legs in the straddle or splits position.

The Thomas flair will normally be learnt on the pommel horse before it is transferred to the floor. The usual sequence for learning the Flair will include:
1. Perfection of double leg circles on the pommel horse.

2. Introduction to the flair on a training aid called a 'mushroom trainer' because of its resemblance to a mushroom.
3. Progression to a pommel horse without handles and then onto the handles.

Only when the flair has perfected with good amplitude on the horse can it be transferred to the floor.

Backward Somersault Stretched with Twist

The stretched backward somersault as described in the section on women's floor exercise in Part 4 is frequently performed by both male and female gymnasts as an essential core skill. However, the more advanced gymnast will include a twist or number of twists around the long axis of the body. The backward somersault with twist is frequently preceded by a round-off, back flip but may also be directly linked with other skills in what is called a 'combination tumble'.

The backward somersault with twist can be learnt on a trampoline, from a trampoline into an adjacent landing pit or in a suitably sprung tumbling situation.

To ensure that complete spatial awareness is established it is advisable to introduce the twist as a 'lazy' (three-quarter) back somersault with half turn to back lie on a safety mat. This can then be

A twisting somersault performed by Diego Hypolito (Brazil).

progressed to a back somersault with half turn to land on the feet. The number of twists is then gradually increased by progressively adding half twists as each stage is perfected.

Remember that once the natural or preferred direction of twist has been established this direction should prevail in all elements involving a twist.

BACKWARD SOMERSAULT WITH TWIST(S) – KEY POINTS

- A high stretched back somersault with controlled rotation is essential.
- The twist is initiated as an aerial twist once the take-off has been completed. For a twist to the left the left arm is quickly dropped to the left side of the body, causing the body to tilt, and the twist commences.
- The other arm is then wrapped across the chest to accelerate the twist.
- The aim is to complete the full twist as the body passes through the vertical inverted position.
- Upon completion of the twist the arms are raised to control the somersault rotation and opened to control the twist rotation in readiness for the landing.
- The feet should land slightly behind the hips to allow the somersault rotation to be arrested.
- The hips, ankles and knees will flex to absorb the impact of the landing and the arms may be opened to stop any remaining twist.
- The number of twists can be increased by increasing the height of the somersault, initiating the twist sooner and adding a more vigorous action with the arms.

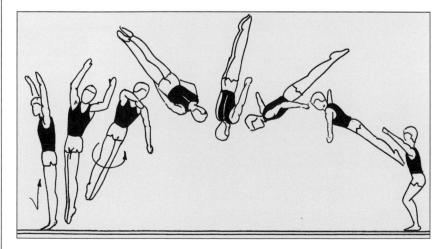

The stretched back somersault with twist on the floor.

Pommel Horse

A routine on pommel horse (or side horse) should include shears or scissor-type elements but skills that include double leg circles must dominate the exercise. Thomas flairs, as illustrated in the floor exercise section, may be included and the routine must conclude with a suitable dismount.

Physical Preparation for Pommel Horse

The pommel horse exercise is one of the most technical and physically demanding of the men's apparatus. Consequently a prerequisite for pommel work is a high level of fitness which includes:

- Upper-body strength to allow the transference of weight from one hand to the other and to support the body as it circles around the hands.
- Mid-body core stability to maintain the tension of the body in the extended position.
- Flexibility and active range in the hips to facilitate the performance of the shears or scissors and flair-type elements.
- Strength endurance to enable a number of demanding circles and pendulum-type swings to be performed without fatigue setting in.

Once the core skills have been learnt, pommel-specific strength endurance can be developed by many repetitions of these skills. It is therefore common to see the gymnasts performing repetitions of shears (eight to ten repetitions) and double leg circles (thirty to forty circles).

The essential skills – shears, double leg circles and the handstand dismount – are described below, together with some key points and training methods. This will provide a broad introduction to the concepts of pommel work.

Forward Shear or Scissors

The forward shear may be developed using the following progressive drills:

FORWARD SHEARS – KEY POINTS

- The forward shear or scissors must be demonstrated with good amplitude, and to achieve this the gymnast must have good flexibility in the hips and good active range leg strength.
- The element commences from a straddled pendulum swing in front support.
- The gymnast transfers his weight sideways on to the support arm (left arm) as the hips and legs swing upwards to the right.
- At the top of the swing the right leg crosses the body of the horse.
- The downward swing continues in the straddled support position and then the left leg dominates the upward swing to the left.
- The weight is transferred onto the right arm, and the lower (right) leg circles backwards under the upper leg before the downward swing commences.
- This constitutes the forward shear to the left. The skill is then repeated to the other side, with the right leg dominating the upward swing to the right and the weight being transferred onto the left arm. The left leg circles backwards under the top (right) leg before the top leg crosses the horse and the forward shear to the right is completed.

---

1. Develop good flexibility in side splits.
2. Achieve active range in leg lifting/leg swinging with both the left and right legs.
3. Straddled leg pendulum swings in front support on the pommel handles.
4. Half forward shear to the left. At the top of the pendulum swing in front

Kristian Berki (Hungary) is a master of the shears on the pommel horse.

support to the right, cross the right leg over the horse and swing down in straddled swing. At the top of the swing to the left, cut the right leg backwards under the left leg and swing downwards in front support.
5. Half forward shear to the right – as above but with the left leg leading.
6. Repetition of half shear to the left and to the right – these drills provide a good basic understanding of the forward shear action. They also help to avoid a common problem where the

The technique for the forward shears.

young gymnasts tend to cut the lead (top) leg across the horse prematurely thus inhibiting the undercut action of the lower leg.

7. Half forward shear to the right into full shear to the right.

8. Half forward shear to the left into full shear to the left.

Once these last two drills have been perfected, combinations of forward shears to the left and right may be introduced.

The gymnast must then learn the technique used to break into the shear from a circling action and also perfect a transfer from the shear into a double leg circle.

A half or full turn may be added into the forward shear to raise the difficulty value of the skill. Another variation is to perform the skill from the top of a backward straddled pendulum swing, and this is known as a backwards shear/scissor.

**DOUBLE LEG CIRCLES –
KEY POINTS**

• The gymnast may perform the circle to the left (circle anticlockwise from back support) or to the right (circle clockwise from the back support position).

• The body must be fully extended (or slightly dished) throughout the circle.

• The body must turn around its long axis in the opposite direction to that of the circle to ensure that the hips face forwards throughout the circle.

• The pattern of the circle is created by the strong pushing and pulling action of the hands against the handles or body of the horse.

• The momentum of the circle is maximized by a powerful drive of the legs from an extended back support position.

• A powerful displacement of the shoulders in a circling motion precedes the circling of the body.

• Since the circle is created by the pulling and pushing action through the hands it is important that the hands are in contact with the horse for maximum time. The hands must therefore be repositioned on to the horse as quickly as possible.

Double Leg Circles

The double leg circle is the most fundamental skill on pommel horse and requires the gymnast to circle with a fully extended body from back support, backwards through side flank support, through front support, then forwards through the opposite side flank returning into back support. The circles may be

Daniel Keatings (GB) circling on the pommel horse.

Some training aids for learning the pommel horse skills.

performed in side support (sideways to the length of the horse) or in cross support (looking along the length of the horse). The hands may be placed on one or both handles or on the body of the horse to give variety and add to the complexity of the skills.

In preparation for the pommel horse circles, the gymnast must develop excellent:

- Mid-body core strength through repetitions of held body shapes, including arched, dished and side flank to the left and right, and log rolls (to do these, start in a held dished position on a box top, then turn around the long axis through held left-side dish, arched back, right-side dish and return to dished position).
- Upper-body support strength by performing front support planche (top planche) in the tucked, straddled and stretched position; and back support Russian levers in the tucked, piked and stretched shape.

A number of training aids are used to develop strength and awareness of the circle and some of these are shown on p.62. When using the floor-level horse the arrangement can be varied to use one or two handles, no handles at all, or even high-density foam blocks that are attached to the body of the horse to replicate the handles. The latter arrangement reduces the risk of injury due to collision with the handles when attempting to learn new skills. Inexperienced gymnasts may tend to dish or pike the body when flanking backwards from the back support position and this should be discouraged since it will cause the hips to turn the wrong way and will reduce the power in the circle. In each stage of learning the gymnast must strive to achieve maximum amplitude in the circle, particularly in the

RIGHT: Louis Smith (GB) dismounting from the pommel horse.

FAR RIGHT: Sebastian Krimmer (Germany) adds a pirouette to the handstand dismount.

back support position and in the rearwards flank phase.

The Handstand Dismount

It is important to finish the routine in a spectacular and stylish manner in order to catch the judge's eye. The most common dismount is a circle or flair into handstand but this must be achieved fluently without the visible use of strength.

To perform the flair or double leg circle into handstand the gymnast must convert the circling motion into a straddled lift to handstand without any noticeable hesitation or obvious strength. This requires great strength and efficiency in the lift to handstand and takes many hours of training to perfect.

The top gymnasts may add a pirouette (a turn in the handstand position), and a travel along the body of the horse to attract a higher difficulty rating for the dismount.

HANDSTAND DISMOUNT – KEY POINTS

- The circle or flair preceding the lift should resemble a slight pendulum circle to begin the conversion from circling to lifting of the hips.
- In an anticlockwise circle the right hand must be rapidly replaced in the back support position and must press down powerfully to convert the circle into lift.
- From the back support position the hips begin to lift as the weight is transferred to the right arm.
- As the left arm is replaced, the shoulders are drawn forward and the legs commence the straddle action.
- The legs are widely separated as the hips are smoothly lifted into the Japana handstand.
- The legs continue to circle sideways and upwards into handstand.
- The handstand should be held for a moment before dismounting to land to the side of the horse.

Rings

A competition routine will include swings both forwards and backwards, into and through the handstand; and lifts or presses into handstand, combined with extraordinary strength parts. The routine must end with a dismount that is commensurate with the difficulty of the exercise. This section will provide an insight into some common rings skills, together with an example of how the amazing strength can be developed.

The Giant Swing

The giant swing commences in the handstand position and requires the gymnasts to swing downwards, passing through the hang position before circling upwards into the handstand position. The skill can be performed in the backwards direction, with the front of the chest leading in the swing, or forwards, where the back of the chest leads the swing.

Before attempting the giant swing the gymnast must be capable of performing a powerful swing in hang and also a stable handstand on slightly swinging rings. The next stage is to perform consecutive, progressively higher 'dislocations' until the gymnast is passing into the handstand position. The downswing from handstand

---

THE BACKWARD GIANT SWING – KEY POINTS

- From the handstand the arms are pressed forwards and slightly open to commence the downswing.
- The chest should lead the downswing and the body should be stretched and tensioned.
- The body is arched through the hang position to stretch the front of the body in readiness for the strong upwards kick of the legs.
- In the first quarter of the upward swing the shoulders remain passive to allow the body to rotate about the shoulders.
- Once the centre of mass is above the line through the shoulders, the rings are pulled backwards and sideways to make the body circle upwards.
- The arms continue to press downwards then inwards as the body circles into the handstand.
- The gymnast must adjust the position of the rings to ensure that the centre of mass remains above the hands to maintain the balance in the handstand.

(some times called the 'bail') into swing and then into high dislocation is then introduced. These drills must be perfected before the full giant is attempted.

Throughout the learning stages the coach will normally provide support through the hang phase, as this is the most

---

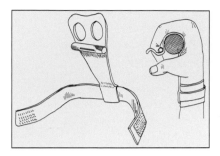

The hand grips used by male gymnasts on the rings.

critical or high risk point of greatest load and momentum.

The gymnast may experience a load seven times their body weight as they swing through the hang position during a giant swing. This is why gymnasts wear a pair of hand guards or grips, which have a dowel peg attached to add to the grip on the rings. The guards are made from pigskin leather and the dowel is either plastic or leather.

The Cross or Crucifix

The cross requires the gymnast to hold a static position with arms horizontal with the rings and the body hanging beneath the shoulders. The traditional cross is performed with an extended body but it can also be shown in the half lever or piked position.

These elements should only be attempted by mature gymnasts as they place great demands on the muscles. It takes many months of strenuous training to develop sufficient strength to perform these very demanding positions. The coach will devise a range of progressively more demanding exercises, which may include the following circuit of exercises:

1. From support, lower into the position (eccentric strength) and press back to the support position (concentric strength). Repeat the exercise three times.
2. From support, lower into the position and hold for between 3 and 7 seconds (isometric strength). Then lower to hang (eccentric strength) and then circle up or muscle up to support. Repeat three times.

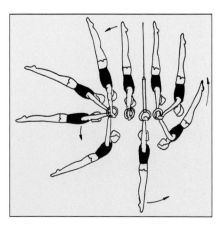

The technique for the backward giant swing on the rings.

Thomas Tarana (Germany) swinging on the rings.

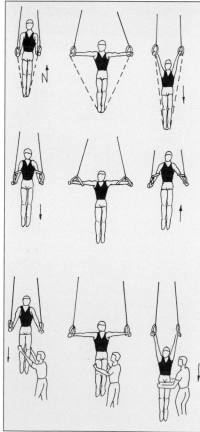

ABOVE LEFT: Oleksandr Vorobiov (Ukraine) holds an impressive cross on the rings.

ABOVE: Jordan Jovtchev (Bulgaria) shows the half lever version of the cross.

LEFT: Exercises for developing the strength for performing the cross. The first illustration shows an elastic strand being used to reduce the load and the second uses looped rings to shorten the lever and thus reduce the load. The final image shows how the coach may provide assistance, which will gradually reduce as the gymnast gains in confidence and strength.

3. Lower slowly from support, through the cross position into the hang position (eccentric strength), muscle up to support and repeat three times.

Usually three sets of the circuit are performed three times per week, and the level of demand is gradually increased as the gymnast gains in strength. The circuit described above can be performed in various situations as shown in the illustrations.

The Johnasson

This skill commences with a powerful swing rearwards in hang followed by double piked somersault above ring height with a smooth transition back into a swing in hang.

The prerequisites for this skill are the ability to perform a powerful swing in hang and front somersaults in the tucked

The Johnasson performed by Kohei Uchimura.

THE JOHNASSON – KEY POINTS

- From a powerful downswing the body is fully extended through the hang position.
- The legs are driven backwards and upwards but the shoulders remain down and are passive.
- As the centre of mass rises above the shoulders, and with the legs approaching shoulder height, the rings are pressed open and the hips are lifted into a pike.
- This reduces the resistance to rotation and the piked body begins to quickly circle forwards and upwards.
- The rings remain to the side but without support as the body continues into a double piked somersault.
- As the body begins to descend the rings are pressed rearwards and the body extends.
- The shoulders and upper back should lead in the smooth transition into the downward swing.
- The arms should be parallel in the later phase of the downswing and the shoulder angle must gradually open to ensure a smooth hang phase.

DOUBLE BACK SOMERSAULT WITH TWIST – KEY POINTS

- The somersault must have good elevation above ring height.
- The tucked shape must be slightly open to reduce the resistance to twist rotation.
- The degree of somersault rotation must therefore be greater than for a tightly tucked double somersault to compensate for the more open body shape.
- The twist will be introduced as an aerial twist using a tilt twist technique.
- The rings are pressed open before being released on the upswing.
- To create a twist to the left the right arm is momentarily raised and the left shoulder is pulled backwards and downwards.
- The right arm is then wrapped quickly across the chest to accelerate the twist.
- The body is then gradually extended and the arms raised and opened to control the twist and somersault rotation in preparation for the landing.

and piked position. The skill may be taught in the tucked position before progressing to the piked version.

The initial attempts may involve a degree of support on the rings during the second somersault, but this should be gradually phased out as awareness and confidence increases.

Ring Dismounts

Most top gymnasts will conclude the routine with a forwards or backwards double somersault performed in the tucked, piked or stretched position. The dismount may also include one or more twists in the double somersault.

This advanced skill will be taught over a long period of time and developed through a series of progressions which may include the following drills:

1. A familiarity with double somersaults developed on the trampoline or from the trampoline into a landing pit.
2. The tucked double back somersault dismount onto a safety mat consistently performed.
3. High double tucked back somersault progressing to an open tucked double somersault dismount into a landing pit.
4. Progressively add a half then full twist to the double somersault to land in the landing pit.
5. As confidence and awareness increases, the dismount is performed onto safety mats in the landing pit and the mats gradually raised in height until level with the floor.
6. The dismount is then practised to land on a safety mat placed upon the normal competition landing surface with the coach spotting the landing.

At the higher performance levels gymnasts often dismount with a double straight back somersault, sometimes with one or two twists added.

Samuel Offord (Australia) dismounting with a double back somersault with added twist.

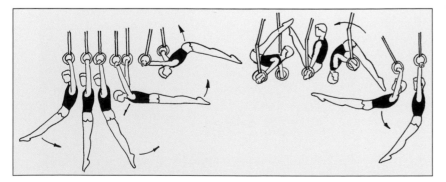

The technique used in the Johnasson.

TECHNICAL SKILLS IN MEN'S GYMNASTICS 69

Vault

Vaulting in men's gymnastics is similar to that in women's gymnastics but the height of the vaulting table is raised to 1.35m. Each vault is given a particular reference number and tariff according to the category and difficulty of the vault. The vaults are classified according to the manner in which the vault commences and broadly the groups are:

Handspring vaults Handspring vault, handspring with twist and handspring with one or more somersaults

Round-off on top of the table Tsukahara vault and Kasamatsu vault, to which one or more twists may be added.

Round-off onto the springboard followed by a backward handspring into a Yurchenko vault or a half turn into a forward handspring-type vault.

THE TSUKAHARA VAULT – KEY POINTS

- The gymnast approaches the vault with a dynamic run-up and fast but low trajectory onto the table.
- The hands must reach quickly to the horse in order to maintain the momentum from the take-off.
- The first hand is rotated through 90 degrees and the arm is flexed to permit a rapid placement of the second hand, which is rotated through around 120 degrees.
- The body and legs rotate about the hands and the body makes a half turn into the handstand.
- The round-off is followed by a powerful push from both hands through the handstand position.
- This thrust from the arms is synchronized with a kick of the feet to set up a 'snapping' action from the top of the table.
- This 'snap-up' causes the shoulders to lift upwards and backwards and the body begins to rotate about the centre of mass.
- The arms are pressed into the thighs to reduce the resistance to rotation and the shoulders are lifted into an arched backward somersault.
- The body is then dished and the arms are lifted to reduce the rotation in preparation for the landing.
- The legs should arrive on the floor behind the hips to enable the somersault rotation to be arrested.
- The ankles, knees and hips are flexed to absorb the impact on landing.

The Tsukahara vault technique.

Kohei Uchimura adds a twist to the Tsukahara vault.

Some examples of these vaults and how they can be developed are described below.

The Tsukahara Vault

The vault consists of a round-off on top of the vaulting table into a stretched one and a quarter backward somersault from the hands.

The difficulty of the basic Tsukahara vault may be increased by adding one or more twists to the somersault as shown in the photograph. The twist may be partially initiated with a slight torque turn through the hands against the table but the majority of the twist should be by means of a tilt twist action. The gymnast will find it easier to control the landing with an aerial twist.

The Handspring Front Somersault Vault

This vault comprises a handspring vault followed by a one and a half front somersault in the second flight phase. This vault, the Roche, is named after Jorge Roche from Cuba who was the first gymnast to perform it, in 1976. This vault requires a powerful thrust from the vaulting table in order to set up good flight and rotation from the hands. The somersault may be performed in the tucked, piked or even in the stretched shape.

The gymnast will normally use drills such as those shown here to develop the technique and awareness required for this vault.

The set-up in the first illustration is designed to help the gymnast develop the powerful thrust from the table and to experience the flight from the table, which must initially be in the stretched shape. The purpose of the second set-up is to enable the gymnast to make the transition from the stretched handspring into the tucked somersault in a safe situation.

The gymnast may then perform the full vault from the vaulting table onto a safety mat placed in a landing pit. The coach may assist the gymnast by supporting on the thighs and mid-back or supporting at the front and back of the waist. The safety mats will then be gradually built up in height up to floor level to allow the gymnast to safely practise the full vault.

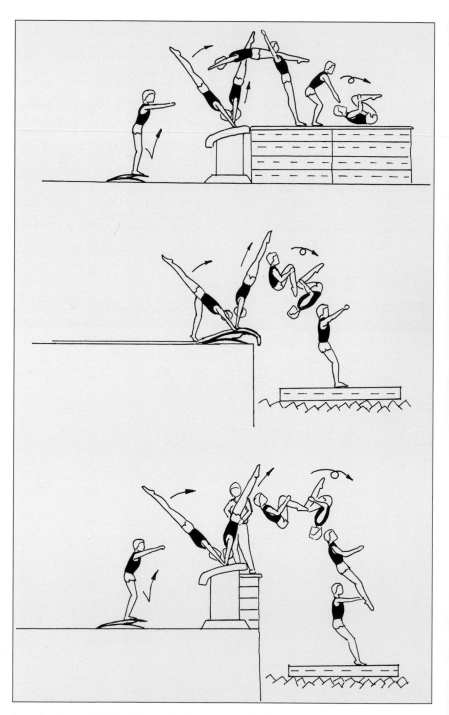

Some development drills for the handspring front somersault vault.

HANDSPRING FRONT SOMERSAULT VAULT – KEY POINTS

- A powerful run-up is translated in a low pre-jump onto the springboard.
- At the take-off the arms are driven forwards to quickly contact the table and the heels are driven upwards. .
- The body may be slightly arched or straight as the hands contact the platform and the gymnast will momentarily rotate about the hands.
- A powerful thrust through the arms and shoulders against the table should occur just before the handstand position.
- A drive of the legs combined with the thrust from the hands produces the high flight path of the centre of mass and creates a large turning effect on the body.
- The body should be fully extended until the point where the hands leave the table.
- The arms then reach quickly upwards to grasp the shins as the gymnast rapidly assumes the tucked position. This reduces the resistance to rotation, and the speed (rotational velocity) of the somersault will increase.
- The tight tucked position is maintained until the start of the last half of the somersault. With the head and shoulders rising, the body begins to extend and the arms are raised to control the rotation in preparation for the landing.
- Upon landing, the feet must be in front of the hips to stop the somersault rotation.
- The ankles, knees and hips flex and the arms are pressed downwards to absorb the impact on landing.

The vault may then be performed onto a safety mat placed on the normal competition landing surface with the coach spotting the landing.

The more powerful gymnasts are able to perform two and a half somersaults from the handspring to create a very difficult and spectacular vault named after Romanian gymnast Marian Dragulescu. He is one of the world's greatest vaulters and is a frequent gold medallist in the vaulting event at major championships. The first photograph shows the immense height that Marian generates to perform the Dragulescu vault.

BELOW LEFT: The master in flight during the Dragulescu vault.

BELOW: Marian Dragulescu celebrates another good vault performance.

Controlling the Landing

The ability to land safely and in control is an essential ingredient of all apparatus dismounts, but in vaulting the landing is paramount. The gymnast must arrest the rotation from the somersault and twist and must control the forwards or backwards momentum to produce a landing without stepping with the feet. The landing must also be in line with the vaulting table.

The vault landing requires great skill and the gymnast will perform the exercises shown below many times in order to perfect the skill.

The coach will set up a variety of stations through which the gymnast can learn to control the landing whilst travelling forwards or backwards with momentum and rotation. The inclusion of a twisting jump, travelling forwards or backwards, will enable the gymnast to learn how to arrest the twist and control the landing.

Drills for the development of secure landings on vault.

> ### SAFE, CONTROLLED LANDINGS – KEY POINTS
>
> - The arms should be raised and the body extended prior to landing to reduce rotation in preparation for the landing.
> - The placement of the feet in relation to the hips and centre of mass is critical to enable a counter-turning effect to be produced against the landing surface. This will allow the forwards or backwards travel and rotation to be reduced to zero.
> - If the gymnast is travelling or rotating forwards the feet must be placed in front of the centre of mass.
> - If the gymnast is travelling or rotating backwards the feet must be positioned behind the centre of mass.
> - If on landing the arms are circled in the opposite direction to the rotation of the body, this will tend to counteract or reduce the rotation.
> - To reduce or remove any twist in the body the arms should be opened wide and turned in the opposite direction to the twist. This will produce a 'counter torque' or opposite turning effect from the floor to remove the twist.

Mathias Fahig of Germany lands with good control from his vault.

Parallel Bars

On this apparatus the gymnast is required to show elements above and below the bars, skills with flight and end the routine with a suitably difficult dismount.

The foundation for parallel bar work is a powerful swing in support; all gymnasts must master this skill with good technique to ensure that the more advanced skills can be safely and correctly learned.

An effective technique for swinging in support on parallel bars.

SWING IN SUPPORT – KEY POINTS

- The body is fully extended upwards in the handstand position to raise the centre of mass.
- The swing is initiated with the feet to move the centre of mass off balance.
- The shoulders are moved forwards slightly and the body extended in the downswing.
- The hips accelerate from horizontal through to the vertical position.
- The shoulders should move backwards to be directly above the hands in the vertical support position and the body is arched.
- The feet and legs are driven upwards whilst the shoulders lean slightly backwards. This shortens the path of the centre of mass and maintains the upward momentum.
- The body should ideally be straight during the forward upswing.
- At the start of the return downswing the body remains stretched and the shoulders move to a position above the hands as the body passes vertical.
- The heels are then accelerated through the vertical support position.
- The shoulders must move forwards in front of the hands to shorten the path of the centre of mass to maintain the momentum in the upswing.
- The body is slightly arched as the heels lead the upswing.
- As the body approaches the vertical line the hands press vigorously forwards against the bars to move the shoulders backwards above the hands. This pushes the centre of mass in an upwards direction, and the body should be straightened to arrest the swing into the handstand position.

As the gymnast becomes stronger and more experienced a powerful swing may be generated to the extent that he will feel the bars lifting upwards during the swing into the handstand position. At this point the gymnast may learn to press against the bars to convert the upswing into a release of the bars and a flight into the handstand. This is a useful technique for learning some advanced parallel bar skills.

The Forward Stutz

The Stutz can be performed on the forwards or backwards swing and is a good example of where a powerful swing in support is put to good effect. The forward Stutz is described here. Essentially it involves a half turn during the forwards upswing with flight into handstand.

A Stutz performed by Danell Leyva of the USA.

THE FORWARD STUTZ – KEY POINTS

- A powerful downward swing is generated from the handstand.
- The body is arched as it passes through the vertical support position and the shoulders should be directly above the hands.
- The gymnast must be relaxed in the shoulders to allow a free swing to occur.
- At the start of the upswing the shoulders will begin to lean slightly backwards as the leg drive is added.
- As the body swings powerfully above the shoulders on the forwards upswing the feet and legs begin to initiate the half turn and a twist appears in the body.
- One arm is released to facilitate the turn around the support hand and the other shoulder moves forwards to be over the support hand.
- With the body approaching the vertical, the gymnast presses downwards and sideways through the support arm to move the centre of mass in between the bars.
- The bar is released and the half turn of the body continues as the gymnast flies into the handstand position.
- Upon re-grasping the bars the gymnast must press down and forwards against the bars and extend the body to arrest the swing into the handstand.

The Tipelt

This is a very complex skill, which requires the gymnast to swing down from handstand into a swing in hang beneath the bars and then use the upward momentum and a powerful press against the bars to counter rotate the body to re-catch above the bars in a straddle position. The gymnast then continues to swing smoothly into the handstand position.

The coach may support the gymnast under the thighs and under the chest as he practises the arched downswing. This technique is needed to control the downswing and to set up the strong snap action in the hips that allows the feet to lead the swing beneath the bars.

Stutz on the parallel bars.

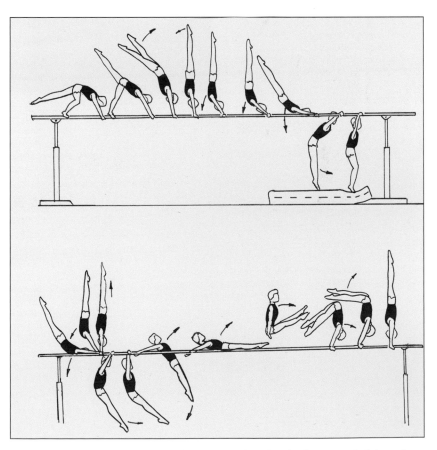

The Tipelt is a common under-bar skill. The first illustration shows how the distinctive arched downswing, or bail, may be learnt, with the coach supporting the gymnast under the thighs and chest. The second illustration shows the complete Tipelt skill.

THE TIPELT – KEY POINTS

- From the handstand the chest leads the downswing and the feet remain momentarily in the vertical position. This produces the strong arch in the downswing
- As the hips approach the line of the bars the gymnast presses strongly against the bars to check the upper body and the legs are vigorously snapped into the piked shape.
- The feet then lead the dished swing in hang beneath the bars.
- The feet are then checked and a vigorous pull backwards and downwards on the bar converts the rotation into a forwards direction. This action also propels the gymnast above the bars.
- During the flight the hips pike to allow the body to rotate forwards and the legs are then straddled.
- The hands re-grasp the bars between the legs, and, with the shoulders leaning forwards, the gymnast performs a smooth straddle lift to handstand.

The Straddled Front Somersault

The straddled front somersault requires a very high flight above the bars to allow a forward one and a quarter somersault in the piked and straddled position to be performed before re-catching the bars in underarm support. This spectacular element requires great courage as well as a high level of technical skill.

This skill can be developed firstly on a trampoline as a one and a quarter straddled pike front somersault to front landing on a slide in safety mat. The gymnast may then transfer to the parallel bars with padding. The element is initially performed as a straddled front somersault to straddle sit on the padded bars. Once the awareness has been established the full skill can be attempted to land in upper arm support on the padded bars. The pads are then removed and the gymnast wears arm pads on their upper arm to protect the arms from the impact of landing on the bars.

ABOVE: *Mitja Petkovsek of Slovenia swings into the Tipelt on parallel bars. The photograph shows the exaggerated downswing technique that is typical in the execution of the skill.*

BELOW: *The technique for the straddled front somersault.*

STRADDLED FRONT SOMERSAULT – KEY POINTS

- A powerful swing must be generated in the downswing.
- The legs are accelerated through the support position with the shoulders directly above the hands.
- At the start of the upswing the gymnast must lean the shoulders forwards in front of the hands to allow the body to rotate quickly about the shoulders.
- The heels are rapidly accelerated into an arched shape and the head is tilted backwards.
- As the centre of mass approaches the vertical position the hands are pressed forwards against the bars to cause the shoulders to move backwards over the hands.
- The centre of mass is directed upwards into the high flight path and the bars are released.
- The feet are then checked and the upper body is accelerated upwards into the straddled pike front somersault.
- Upon completion of the somersault the feet circle backwards as the body extends.
- The hands reach for the bars and the gymnast lands on the bars with the underarms.
- It is important that a strong underarm support is maintained to avoid compression on the sternum.

Fenge Zhe (China) shows great height above the bars in the straddled front somersault.

The Double Piked Back Somersault Dismount

The most common dismounts from the parallel bars include single somersaults, forwards or backwards with and without twists and double somersaults forwards or backwards. Many of the top gymnasts perform the double piked back somersault since this more difficult skill attracts a higher difficulty value.

This advanced skill will be developed through a series of progressive skills and a variety of training aids such as a trampoline and parallel bars placed adjacent to a landing pit. The swing and release technique from the parallel bars can be practised into a high piked somersault to stand or back landing onto a pile of safety mats at bar height. The double tuck, then the double pike back

---

DOUBLE PIKED BACK SOMERSAULT DISMOUNT – KEY POINTS

- The gymnast must develop a dynamic swing through support and carry this into the upswing.
- On the forwards upswing the shoulders lean backwards to permit a fast upswing.
- The legs are driven into an open piked shape as the hips move above the line of the shoulders.
- The hands and arms then press downwards, backwards and sideways against the bars to lift the centre of mass into the sideways and upwards flight path.
- As the hands are released from the bars they swing quickly upwards to grasp behind the thighs and pull the legs into a deep pike to accelerate the somersault.
- The body then extends and the arms are raised to control the rotation in preparation for the landing.
- The feet must be placed just behind the hips on landing, and the ankles, knees and hips flex to allow for a controlled landing.

---

somersaults from the bars will be performed into landing pits and then onto safety mats placed in the pit. The height of the safety mats will be gradually raised to floor level, to simulate the correct relationship between the bars and the landing module. The coach will usually support the gymnast from above and to the side of the bars in the initial learning stages to ensure the correct execution of the technique. Once the dismount has

---

Kohei Uchimura (Japan) dismounting with a double piked back somersault

been consistently and successfully performed onto the safety mats in the pit, the final stage is performing the dismount onto the landing pad. The coach will normally spot the landing until the skill has been perfected.

The double piked somersault dismount from parallel bars.

Horizontal Bar

The horizontal bar is perhaps the most exciting of all the men's gymnastic apparatus. The gymnasts perform forwards and backwards giant swings with intricate turns in connection with close bar skills and amazing release and re-catch elements. The dismount, which must be commensurate with the difficulty of the routine, is often especially spectacular.

The Giant Swing

The foundation skills for horizontal bar work are the forwards and backwards giant swings. In a giant swing the gymnast makes a complete rotation around the bar, commencing in handstand and returning to the handstand. In the forwards giant the back of the torso leads the swing and the hands grasp the bar in 'under-grasp'. The forwards giant was described in Part 4 in the section on asymmetric bars, and the men use similar techniques to those used by the women. In the backwards giant swing the front of the chest leads in the swing and the hands are in 'over-grasp' on the bar. The backward giant is described here.

This essential core skill requires good general physical preparation, particularly

Daniel Keating (GB) adding a twist during the giant swing.

BACKWARDS GIANT SWING –
KEY POINTS

- Commencing in the handstand, extend the body in the first quarter of the downswing to maximize the swing.
- After passing the horizontal line, a 'timing' action is introduced by dishing and kicking the heels backwards.
- The body is stretched into an arch beneath the bar and this pre-stretch of the body allows the kicking action during the hang phase.
- On the upswing, the path of the centre of mass is brought closer to the bar to maintain the momentum of the upswing. This is achieved by dishing the body and closing the shoulder angle.
- Once the centre of mass is above the horizontal line through the bar, the gymnast presses downwards on the bar to open the shoulder angle and to force the centre of mass upwards and over the bar.
- The feet should lead throughout the upswing and the head should remain in a neutral position.
- The body is gradually stretched, arriving in the handstand position in a straight or slightly dished shape.

in the handstand shape. On normal apparatus it is necessary to use hand chalk (magnesium carbonate) to absorb perspiration and ensure the grip is maintained. The gymnast will usually wear hand guards or grips to protect the hands against the friction and heat that is generated between the hands and the apparatus. It takes a considerable time for

the gymnasts to develop sufficiently tough skin on the hands to allow them to swing around the apparatus without blistering or tearing the skin. The giant swing may be learnt on a polished bar (without chalk) with the gymnast being secured to the bar with gloves and loops or loops and a rotating sleeve, as shown in the pictures.

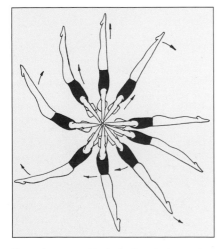

The technique used in the backwards giant swing on horizontal bar.

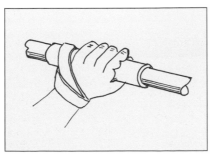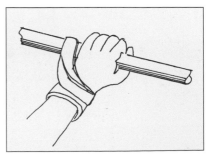

Gloves and loops are often used when learning bar skills to secure the gymnast to the bar.

The set-ups illustrated here allow the young gymnasts to attempt a high number of repetitions of the progressive learning skills without the complication of blistering hands. Gloves, loops and sleeves are a real asset in the learning stages of even advanced skills where the release of the hands is not a requirement.

To learn the giant swing, the gymnast will first perform the dish, arch and dish sequence in a static hang on the bar. This important drill is then included in the swing, which gradually increases in amplitude and momentum until the gymnast generates sufficient swing to pass into the handstand position. It is important that the gymnast understands the technique of re-grasping of the bar as they fall from handstand with the back leading. This will be a very helpful safe outlet

when attempting to learn the giant swing on the chalk bar. From this stage the gymnast is supported by the coach through consecutive giant swings until he can safely and consistently perform the skill unaided.

The giant swing is then transferred to the normal chalked bar with the coach providing appropriate support at each stage of learning. Once the skill is mastered it can be used as an accelerator skill leading into other skills, or various forms of turn around the long axis of the body can be added.

The Kovacs

The Kovacs is one of the most spectacular release and re-catch elements,

performed only by the more skilful gymnasts. The Kovacs is essentially a double back somersault over the bar with a re-catch of the bar. It requires great courage and good spatial awareness as well as a high level of technical skill. The Kovacs is usually performed in the tucked position but some of the more skilled or daring gymnasts will perform it in the piked or even the stretched position. The more common tucked version is described here.

The very best gymnasts may perform the 'kick out' into the stretched position high over the bar to create a greater impression; Kohei Uchimura of Japan is a great exponent of this technique.

OPPOSITE: *Kohei Uchimura (Japan) shows impeccable style during stretched Kovacs.*

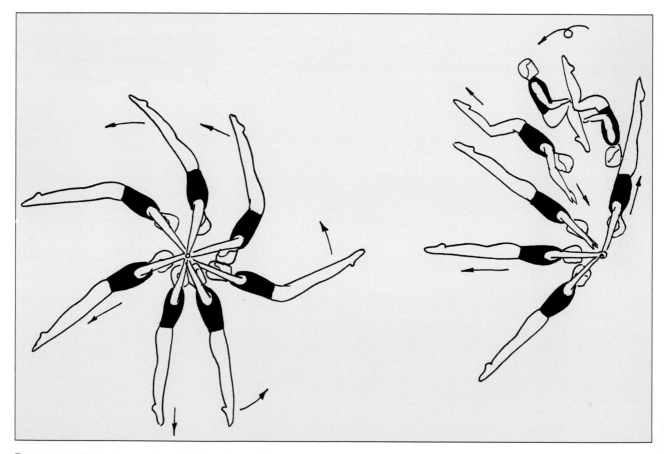

The spectacular Kovacs release and re-catch skill on horizontal bar.

THE KOVACS – KEY POINTS

- The Kovacs is preceded by an accelerated giant swing.
- The gymnast dishes across the bar to increase the speed in the last phase of the giant swing.
- The gymnast enters the downswing in a distinct dish shape and maintains the shape until passing under the bar.
- This has the effect of pulling the bar downwards, storing energy in it.
- The gymnast then momentarily arches before kicking the legs upwards into a dished shape again.
- As the handstand is approached the energy stored in the bar from the earlier downward bend is now returned and the gymnast quickly extends the body above the bar.
- The bar is released just before the vertical, creating a flight path upwards and over the bar.
- The gymnast quickly tucks and grasps the shins to accelerate the rotation into the somersault phase.
- The gymnast then snaps the body into the straight shape to slow down the rotation in preparation for the re-grasp of the bar.

The Double Layout Back Somersault Dismount

Dismounts from the horizontal bar will include single stretched somersaults at a basic level through to double somersaults with and without twists. The triple somersault is also performed by some advanced gymnasts. The double layout back somersault is a popular dismount for experienced gymnasts.

This dismount can be developed from a double tucked somersault dismount by the following sequence of drills:

1. Double layout somersault from a trampoline into a pitted landing area.
2. One and a quarter stretched somersault dismount from the bar to back landing on a safety mat in a landing pit.
3. Double open tucked dismount into landing pit.
4. Progress to the double layout into the landing pit then onto safety mats placed in the pit.

5. Gradually raise the height of the safety mats to floor level.
6. Transfer the dismount to the competition landing surface with safety mat on the landing pad.
7. The coach will shadow the performance and spot the landing in these later stages to ensure the safety of the gymnast.

The more daring and skilful gymnasts may add one or more twists into the double layout dismount to increase the value.

DOUBLE LAYOUT BACK SOMERSAULT DISMOUNT – KEY POINTS

- The dismount is preceded by a powerful and accelerated backward giant swing.
- The body is dished over the bar to increase the speed of the swing.
- The body is extended into an arch below the bar.
- The legs are kicked dynamically into a dished shape at the start of the upswing.
- The shoulder angle is closed to maintain the momentum of the upswing.
- With the feet directly above the shoulders and the centre of mass just above the bar, the bar is released.
- After releasing the bar the shoulders are lifted upwards and backwards into an arched or straight position.
- The arms are driven towards the thighs to maximize the rotation.
- Upon completion of one and one half somersaults the body is dished and the arms lifted to control the rotation in preparation for the landing.

ABOVE: The technique used in the double layout back somersault dismount.

LEFT: Kristian Thomas (GB) twists with ease in the double layout dismount.

PART 6
SUSTAINING PERFORMANCE

The complexity of the training and competition programme places huge physical and psychological demands on gymnasts. To ensure that they have the best chance of a long and successful career, it is necessary that coaches provide for the welfare and safety of the gymnasts and take a holistic approach to their long-term development. As the gymnasts mature and gain experience, coaches must be able to amend their coaching style in order to meet the individual needs of the gymnasts. At the higher performance levels, the coach or programme manager will secure the services of support staff, such as sports psychologists, biomechanists, physiotherapists and nutritionists to advise the coaches and support the gymnasts. However, it is advisable that all coaches and their gymnasts have a good understanding of these topics and rigorously apply this knowledge and advice to the training. Each of these topics is explained in this part of the book.

The Role of the Coach and Coaching Styles

The role of the gymnastics coach is multi-faceted and will incorporate many inter-related skills and competencies. Some of these have been described elsewhere in this book. The primary role of the coach is to create an environment that will enable the gymnasts to achieve their ultimate potential. The relationship between the coach and gymnast will vary over time but it will inevitably have to be based upon mutual trust if the relationship is to be sustained. A coach may oversee the progression of a gymnast from being a young child prodigy all the way through to becoming a mature adult gymnast. As the gymnasts mature and gain experience the relationship and style of coaching will need to change as the gymnasts are empowered to take a greater responsibility for their training and lifestyle.

To fully understand the intricacies of the various coaching styles it is helpful if we understand the process through which the gymnasts learn the gymnastic skills.

The gymnast and coach have mutual trust in each other.

How Gymnastic Skills are Learned

Gymnastic skills are generally learned after many repetitions of progressive part and whole skills, but the learning will take place through three distinct stages:

Cognitive stage In the early stages of learning the gymnast will be concerned with which movements are required in order to understand the skill. Errors will be large and the performance will be erratic. The gymnast will require frequent feedback and guidance to help them make progress.

Associative stage In this stage the gymnast will begin to refine the movements as they have more understanding of the skill. Errors will be smaller and less frequent and changes will be more refined. During this stage of learning the coach should provide feedback after a small number of attempts at the skill. The gymnast should be encouraged to self-evaluate the performances and begin to find solutions for improving the performance.

Autonomous stage The movements will eventually become automatic and the skill is said to have become 'overlearned'. The skill will continue to improve and be consolidated with just very fine changes being made. Feedback should be provided infrequently and usually given after a whole series of attempts. The gymnast may make subtle adjustments as they refine the performance and the coach will monitor the performance to ensure that the intended pattern of movement is not lost.

Coaching Styles

The stages of learning and feedback requirements described above apply whatever level the gymnast is at. However, as the gymnast matures and becomes more experienced the style of coaching may need to be varied in accordance with the age, personality and experience of the individual gymnast. The styles of coaching are generally broadly classified as autocratic, democratic and authoritarian.

The autocratic coach The autocratic coach will offer frequent instructions and feedback in a manner similar to that of a parent in a parent to child relationship. The coach will make all the decisions concerning the performance and the development of the gymnasts.

The democratic coach The coach will relate to the gymnast in an adult-to-adult manner and will invite the performer to discuss and comment on all aspects of their training and development. The coach will provide less frequent feedback but encourage the gymnast to evaluate the performance and provide their views on solutions for improving their performance. The coach should frequently check that the gymnast is on the right track by asking pertinent questions and analysing the gymnast's responses.

The authoritarian coach This type of coach demands respect and obedience and expects results. They are usually well organized and meticulous in their planning. The disciplined environment is often conducive to positive training and often leads to success. Introverted, sensitive and less confident participants may however feel threatened and deterred by this approach.

The coach and gymnast discussing strategies.

When working with very young gymnasts it is more usual to adopt an autocratic/authoritarian approach to start with, since frequent information and feedback is required to help them to understand the fundamental skills. This approach may also establish the discipline and set the benchmark for the work ethic that will be required through out the gymnast's career. It is important, however, not to rely entirely on the 'tell' style of coaching as the gymnasts will learn more quickly if they are encouraged to think for themselves. The coach will begin to challenge the gymnasts by asking them to comment on their own or even their peers' performance. In time the participants will be able to recognize good and not so good performances and will be able to offer solutions to problems. This creates a greater focus on the performance and allows the coach to gauge the level of understanding.

The key to a successful coaching relationship is to adapt the style of coaching to meet the needs of the individual gymnasts at each stage of their development. As the gymnasts mature and become more experienced the democratic style of coaching should predominate. However, when new skills are being introduced, the gymnast will require frequent information and an autocratic approach may be advisable. The coach should endeavour to develop the self-confidence of the gymnasts so that they eventually become self-sufficient and not reliant on the coach for support.

Providing Instruction and Feedback

Good communication is an essential ingredient of coaching: the coach must be able to provide clear instruction and accurate feedback. The coach must also be able to observe and analyse a gymnastic performance and then provide the gymnast with accurate constructive feedback to help to improve the performance. This can be a difficult skill to develop, but the following techniques are a useful guide.

- Observe and memorize the performance.
- Make a mental comparison with a model of an optimum performance.
- Use a cause and effect approach to identify the outcome (the effect) and action (the cause) that may have produced a defect in the performance.
- Allow a few seconds for the gymnast to come out of performance mode and into self-analysis mode. This also gives the coach time to analyse the performance.
- Discuss the outcome, cause and effect with the gymnast, encouraging them to rate the performance and provide solutions.
- The coach should provide feedback in the form: praising effort – constructive instruction (one or two key points) – positive praise.
- Focus attention on the key points by practising a related drill or mental rehearsal.
- Just prior to the next approach to the apparatus, question the gymnast about the key points to focus attention on the next performance.

This approach has been proven to be very successful as it creates a positive training environment that continually maintains the focus of the gymnast on the immediate task.

Sports Psychology

It may be assumed that all gymnasts have a desire to achieve their personal aims, but at the higher performance levels the factors that separate the best from the rest are often the commitment, determination and mental preparedness, rather than native ability. It is therefore a huge benefit to the gymnast if they understand and can apply the principles of psychology to the training and competition environment.

Sports performance can be significantly affected by a range of psychological factors, including self-confidence, self-esteem, stress and anxiety. Self-confidence is higher if the gymnast believes that they have the ability to succeed or achieve their goals. Self-esteem is related to how the gymnast sees himself/herself as being respected by his/her peers or coach.

Motivation

Motivation is a key element in the endeavour to reach the desired level of performance, and loss of motivation will have a negative effect on desire and determination. There are two forms of motivation, external motivation and intrinsic motivation.

External motivation is supplied by someone else, for example if the coach uses incentives such as prizes or medals as rewards for winning. The danger with this is that the gymnast will feel they have failed if they do not win and motivation may consequently be lessened.

On the other hand, if the gymnast is encouraged to set realistic goals they will gain in self-esteem and confidence by achieving those goals through their own effort. They will also be more motivated towards achieving their goals. This is intrinsic motivation and comes from within the gymnast. The coach will inevitably encourage the gymnasts to self-motivate, since this has been proven to be more successful and will increase feelings of competence and self-belief in the gymnast.

Motivation may also be enhanced by the coach (and gymnast) adopting the following strategies:

Reward effort The coach can reward the gymnast through praise for the level of effort rather than just for success at achieving a goal.

Making the training interesting and enjoyable Vary the training programme and progressively challenge the gymnasts.

Setting effective goals Realistic, achievable and challenging goals that require the application of suitable effort to achieve them will be highly motivational. It is important to involve the gymnast in setting the goals since this will give feelings of ownership and will increase the desire and determination to achieve.

Positive style of coaching The coach should focus on the effort and good aspects of the gymnast's performance, not solely on what was not so good. Providing feedback in the sequence praise – corrective feedback – praise will prove more positive in maintaining the motivation.

Self-evaluation The coach can encourage the gymnast to evaluate their own performance before providing feedback to the gymnast. This will enable the coach to check that the gymnast is aware of his or her performance and will ensure that the gymnast is more focused on their performance. This will lead to greater confidence and more positive training.

Stress

If a person feels threatened by a situation they will feel anxious, and this may result in them becoming stressed. Some gymnasts may have a general tendency to become anxious (trait anxiety) in a stressful situation and may try to avoid these situations as they expose their weaknesses. The causes of anxiety may include fear of risk of failure, fear of injury, over-zealous coaches or parents, peer pressure, fear of competition and unrealistic goals. Anxiety may lead to stress, and the symptoms of stress include worry thoughts, high excitement, fast pulse, desire for the toilet, weakness in muscles, muscle tension and sweating.

Others may use the event to raise their emotions (state anxiety) and may relish the challenge. A suitable level of stress may therefore improve performance but an excess of anxiety and stress will lead to underperformance. Signs that indicate the gymnast is in the zone and ready to perform are slight excitement, confidence, alertness, keenness and high levels of concentration.

The gymnast Bjorn Slanvall (Sweden) is alert and ready to perform.

Psychological Tools

Psychological training can help the gymnast develop skills and strategies that allow them to control or cope with the factors that influence performance. Some strategies and skills are given here.

Positive Self-Talk
The coach can provide positive feedback and this can be converted into a positive statement that the gymnast can repeat or view to improve focus and increase confidence. This 'positive self-talk' can help to block out negative thoughts that may undermine confidence and hinder performance.

Goal Setting
The gymnast and coach can together prepare and agree targets or goals that will help to guide and motivate the gymnast. The goals must relate to the long-term aims and should be set according to the SMARTER principle:

Specific Clear, precise, understood and agreed by both the gymnast and the coach.

Measurable To clearly indicate when the goal has been achieved.

Adjustable Able to be adjusted if necessary.

Relevant Related to the long-term goals.

Time-based To be completed or achieved by a specific date.

Exciting Challenging and achievable goals.

Realistic In the control of the gymnast and achievable with effort.

Mental Rehearsal
The gymnast can learn to mentally visualize a good performance to boost their confidence and enhance their ability to learn the skill. This can be done in three ways:

External imagery A visual image of the gymnast performing a skill or routine as someone else would see them.

Internal imagery A visual image as the gymnast would see themselves performing.

Proprioceptive imagery The gymnast feels the movement in the muscles as if they were performing the skill or sequence.

Cognitive Restructuring

The mental rehearsal techniques can be used to review a poor performance up until the point where the sequence broke down, and then a successful ending can be added. The successful performance of the whole sequence is repeated until the gymnast is confident that they can perform the skill without a breakdown.

Relaxation

The gymnast can learn techniques to regulate their mental and physical state. Physical relaxation can be achieved through progressive tensioning and relaxing the muscles. A good way to relax mentally is to listen to favourite or baroque music. The gymnast may also focus attention on the breathing

movement of the diaphragm to help them to relax. This technique is called 'centring', and takes the attention away from distracting thoughts.

Concentration Cues

To enable the gymnast to focus their attention on a particular aspect of the performance, different types of cues can be used and these may include:

Visual cues Seeing or spotting a particular point on a wall or floor.

Verbal cues Saying useful words, such as speed, power, smooth, fast and so on.

Physical cues Taking a deep breath and exhaling or tensioning and relaxing muscles.

'What if' Scenarios

Events at a competition do not always go according to plan, and a range of situations can arise that might impact on the gymnast's performance. It is important that the gymnast is suitably prepared to help them to make their own appropriate decisions and to develop strategies that will allow them to deal with a range of eventualities.

During the competition phase of the training programme the gymnast can prepare for the competition by imagining the event arena and mentally rehearsing their performance in the arena. The coach can introduce various intrusions, or 'what if' scenarios, which are intended to break the concentration or interrupt the performance. These might include:

- A sudden loud noise or crowd disturbance designed to disturb concentration.
- The judge signifying their readiness and then deliberately interrupting the gymnast's pre-performance regime.
- Simulating a faulty apparatus situation.
- The judge awarding deliberately incorrect scores.
- A failure of the lighting system.

Through this experience the gymnast will learn how to deal appropriately with unexpected situations and not allow the interruption to affect their performance.

Rebecca Bross (USA) prepares mentally for the asymmetric bars.

The psychological strategies and skills described above may take some time to master and the coach will be wise to build time into the training programme to allow the gymnasts to learn and perfect the skills.

Nutrition and the Energy Systems

When gymnasts exercise they expend energy, and if the energy is not replenished the body will experience fatigue and underperform. Energy is derived from the food we eat through the digestive system and the body transportation systems.

The nutrients in the food are converted into energy by a series of biochemical reactions, and the sources of energy, glycogen and glucose, are stored in the muscles and liver. These substances are broken down into the immediately useable form of energy known as adenosine triphosphate (ATP) through various forms of exercise. The type of exercise undertaken will determine the process through which the energy source (ATP) is released and used. It is therefore important to understand how the type of exercise affects the release of energy and how this in turn influences the food the gymnast must consume.

Types of Exercise and Energy Release

The two types of exercise are briefly described below. Gymnastic training and competition events are predominantly anaerobic in nature but aerobic fitness must also be trained to sustain the general endurance fitness of the gymnasts.

Aerobic Exercise
During low-intensity exercise the glycogen stored in the muscles and liver is broken down in the presence of oxygen into ATP to supply the energy to the muscles. This energy release process can be sustained for long periods of light exercise such as distance running or light endurance

training. Aerobic fitness underpins all forms of training and it is necessary to include this type of activity in the gymnastics programme.

Anaerobic Exercise
As the intensity of the exercise increases the threshold for the aerobic (with oxygen) energy release system is exceeded and the need for instant energy release is provided by the reserve anaerobic (without oxygen) system. The anaerobic system does not require oxygen to release the supply of ATP. It uses the energy resources stored in the muscles.

The anaerobic energy release system can only be sustained for short periods of up to 45 seconds of intensive exercise before fatigue sets in. A side effect of anaerobic activity is the build up of lactic acid in the muscles, leading to fatigue in the muscles and general discomfort. A warm-down or cool-down session of low-level activity is essential following bouts of anaerobic exercise. This will help to disperse the lactic acid and will also start the process of energy recovery.

In order to maximize the anaerobic fitness of the gymnast, training must comprise bouts of exercise of high-intensity exercise lasting between 45 seconds and 1 minute. This is followed by rest periods of 3 to 5 minutes.

These principles must form the basis of both the technical training and physical preparation training sessions to gain maximum benefits.

Nutrition

A complete and balanced diet will include carbohydrates, proteins, fats, minerals, vitamins and liquids, all of which are essential for the efficient functioning of the body. Each of these constituents has a specific function and can be sourced from specific foods.

Carbohydrates
These the main source of energy and can be obtained from wholemeal bread, pasta, beans, pulses, cereals, vegetables, nuts and sugar. Apples and bananas contain

fructose, a form of energy source but without fat.

The normal recommended daily carbohydrate intake for men is around 250–350g per day and for women 150–300g.

The energy expenditure of high performance gymnasts is quite high, however, and the required daily carbohydrate intake can be calculated as follows:

Low intensity training: 6 × body weight in kg = g of carbohydrate per day

High intensity training: 8 × body weight in kg = g of carbohydrate per day
For example, a gymnast with a body weight of 55kg involved in high-intensity exercise would require 440g (8 × 55) of carbohydrate per day to sustain the energy supply.

The rate at which carbohydrates can be digested and absorbed varies with each food, and this is extremely important to bear in mind when a quick carbohydrate boost is required. The speed at which the carbohydrate can be absorbed and the glucose made available is represented by an index called the glycaemic index (GI).
- Foods with a high GI (that is, the glucose is available quickly) include pineapple, bread, watermelon, jelly beans, baked potato, cornflakes, sports drinks and glucose.
- Medium GI foods are muesli, banana, boiled potato, boiled rice, orange juice, and rye bread.

Proteins
Proteins are required by the body to build and repair body tissue, such as muscle cells and haemoglobin. It is recommended that protein is obtained through the consumption of white meats such as chicken and turkey or fish and low-fat dairy products. Protein is also available via red meats, but these tend to contain more fat, which may tend to increase body weight.

Fats
Fats are a source of energy, are used for insulating the body against cold and also protect the vital organs of the body. Eaten in excess, however, they will also increase body weight, so it is recommended that

the energy sourced from fats should not exceed 40 per cent of the total daily energy intake in the diet.

Vitamins and Minerals

Vitamins are classified as vitamins A, B, C, D, E, F and K and are available from fruits, liver, vegetables and dairy products. Vitamins perform specific functions, such as the metabolism of carbohydrates and protein as well as helping the body to heal or resist infection.

Minerals are chemicals that are required for the normal functioning of the body, most importantly:

- Calcium for bone development.
- Iron for the formation of haemoglobin in the blood.
- Sodium and potassium to facilitate the transmission of signals from the nervous system to the muscles.
- Fluoride to maintain the structure of teeth.

A normal balanced diet will include sufficient minerals, and supplements are not usually required.

Fluids

Water is very important for the transportation mechanisms in the body, carrying nutrients to the tissues and eliminating waste products. Water also helps to maintain the body's temperature by absorbing the heat produced through exercise and transporting this to the skin for cooling. This causes sweating, and the heat is lost by evaporation of the sweat.

If the water loss is not replenished the performance may deteriorate and the body may dehydrate.

The Gymnast's Diet

A normal balanced diet is generally recommended but the high-performance gymnast is like a highly tuned racing car that requires the correct fuel in order to function efficiently. Consequently it is necessary to consider a number of factors when advising on the dietary intake for the gymnast.

Calorific intake Most gymnastic training is anaerobic in nature and this does not readily accommodate the metabolism of fat into energy. The gymnast must be lean and powerful and therefore the gymnast's intake of fat will be less than that of a normal person. For the gymnast's diet the recommended proportions for the energy-providing foods are: carbohydrates 62 per cent; protein 16 per cent; fat 22 per cent of the total calorific intake.

Vitamins and minerals It is essential that the recommended daily allowance (RDA) for vitamins and minerals is met, but this can normally be achieved through a good balanced diet of quality foods.

Fats Gymnasts should follow a low-fat diet but this must contain essential fatty acids.

Liquids It is recommended that gymnasts drink small volumes of sucrose/carbohydrate drinks or water frequently during training. Ideally 200–300ml of fluid should be drunk regularly every 15–20 minutes rather than larger volumes at one time.

Training Sessions and Competitions

Generally the intake of carbohydrates should be evenly distributed throughout the day but the gymnast will have specific dietary needs prior to training or competing. Before training or competition the ideal pattern of carbohydrate intake should be as follows:

3–4 hours before the event: 5g of carbohydrate per kg of body weight.

1 hour before the event: 2g of high-GI carbohydrate food per kg of body weight and 300–500ml of carbohydrate drink.

15–20 minutes before the event: High-GI carbohydrate snack or carbohydrate drink.

During the event, to maintain hydration and minimize fatigue, the gymnasts should drink 100–200ml of water or water containing a 6–8% carbohydrate solution every 10–15 minutes.

The best time to replenish the energy stores is within 2 hours of the completion of the exercise, and it is recommended that high-GI foods and carbohydrate drinks are consumed as soon as possible

after the event. The recommended rates are 200–400 calories in the first 2 hours followed by 200–300 calories in the next few hours.

Maintaining Body Weight

High-performance, competitive gymnasts must maintain a fairly lean body in order to perform efficiently and to reduce the risk of injury. The percentage of body fat is a measure of the fat on the body, and this would normally be lower in the trained gymnast than the untrained person.

During childhood and adolescence the body changes significantly and frequently, and measuring body fat to indicate the leanness of the young gymnasts is almost pointless and not recommended. Once beyond the adolescent stage, the percentage body fat of the trained female gymnast would normally be between 14–18 per cent and that of the males 8–10 per cent.

The percentage of body fat can be accurately measured using skin fold callipers together with a scientific calculation involving total body mass and fat free weight. The measure of the total body weight using weighing scales alone is not a reliable indicator of percentage of body fat and this practice is not recommended.

In some training regimes it is common practice to measure the gymnast's total body weight daily, before and after training. This should be done at the same time each day to ensure that the conditions are as near as possible the same on each occasion. In this case the gymnast's ideal or comfortable training and competition weight should have been scientifically determined. The measurement of the body weight before and after the session will indicate the loss of fluid during the training or event. A loss of more than 3 per cent of body weight would be cause for concern if it is not replenished with 48 hours, since this may lead to severe dehydration illness. A loss of just 2 per cent of body mass through fluid loss can lead to a considerable loss in performance.

Where it is identified that a gymnast would benefit by reducing their body weight, this can be achieved by careful manipulation of the diet. Quite simply, if you consume more calories than you use you will gain body weight and if you burn off more than you intake you will lose weight. It is strongly recommended that the advice of a trained and suitably qualified dietician or nutritionist is sought to ensure that appropriate adjustments are made. Ideally the diet would be adjusted to achieve a loss of no more than 1kg a week.

The need to lose body weight is a highly sensitive issue, particularly with young females, and the matter should be handled with great care. On no account should the coach publicly state that a gymnast needs to lose weight. It should be discussed in a private and sensitive manner between the coach, gymnast and parents, and if possible in the presence of a dietician or nutritionist.

Preventing Under-Performance

One of the most important factors in achieving consistent high levels of performance is to achieve the correct balance between the training load and the rest and recovery period.

In order to improve performance the coach will systematically and gradually increase the training load in the gymnast's programme to stimulate adaptation to the imposed demands. This is commonly referred to as the SAID principle. If the training load and recovery are appropriate then the performance levels will rise accordingly. However, if the loading is excessive or sufficient recovery time is not allocated then the gymnast will begin to fatigue and performance levels will drop. This over-training syndrome is often called 'burnout'. The symptoms of burnout in gymnasts are:
- Fatigue
- Loss of drive and determination
- Heavy muscles
- Loss of energy

The typical lean and powerful physique of the modern female gymnast.

- Mood changes
- Loss of appetite accompanied by weight loss
- A rise in resting pulse rate.

The coach must be constantly alert to ensure that any of these symptoms are detected as early as possible. If they are identified, the coach must rectify the situation by reducing the stress factors within and outside the training, allowing adequate rest and light exercise until the recovery is complete and ensuring that a good, balanced diet is maintained.

Burnout is not confined to the gymnasts, and it is also possible that a coach might experience 'coach burnout'. Possible causes of coach burnout are:
- Multiple roles and role conflict
- Excessive coaching and administration hours
- Intense personal involvement
- The pressure to achieve or win medals
- Interference by the administration or parents
- Extensive travel to events.

Research has shown that caring and people-oriented coaches may be more vulnerable to coach burnout. The situation may be addressed by reviewing the time commitments, discussing the issues with a trusted colleague or friend, practising self-regulating skills such as relaxation and positive self-talk, delegating responsibilities and perhaps reviewing the training programme to share the responsibilities.

It is important that both the coach and gymnast have a healthy and appropriate lifestyle in order to cope with the internal and external demands that will affect their well-being.

Prevention and Treatment of Injuries

Artistic gymnastics is generally regarded as a high-risk sport, due to the complex nature of the skills. Despite this classification, the number of serious injuries within the sport is remarkably low. This may be largely due to the coaches taking their duty of care responsibilities very seriously. Every coach must be mindful of the gymnast's health, safety, welfare and general well-being in all their coaching and planning.

Despite the high quality of coaching generally prevalent in gymnastics, accidents will still happen. This section identifies the types of injury that occur and how the injury can be managed. It is intended to be an overview and not an in-depth guide: if there is any doubt whatsoever regarding the seriousness of an injury it is imperative that medical advice is sought.

The factors that have a bearing on how likely it is an injury will occur include:
- **The nature of the sport** The gymnast is required to perform many repetitions of the complex skills and this has an inherent risk of injury.
- **Environment** Good-quality apparatus, training aids and landing surfaces can reduce the possibility of an injury occurring.
- **Physiology of the gymnast** If the level of strength and fitness of the gymnast is not sufficiently high the risk of injury will increase. Physical defects such as poor

posture and misaligned limbs may also raise the risk of injury.
- **Pubescent growth periods** During the period of greatest growth a number of factors can affect the young gymnasts, as the body shape and proportions change and the rate of bone growth exceeds that of the muscles. Together, these result in a loss in flexibility and co-ordination and a reduction in performance. The growth plate areas of bone are at risk of injury due to the repetitive loading.
- **Forces acting on the body** Gymnastic training will cause a range of force effects on the structure of the body. These include tension, compression, shear, bend and torsion, each of which has the potential to cause injury.

Common Gymnastic Injuries

- **Ligaments** The function of the ligaments is to stabilize the joints. Often, poor landings cause the sprain or, in extreme cases, the rupture of the ligaments. Typical accidents include the inversion of the ankle (turning the ankle outwards) resulting in damage to the lateral ligament, and rotational stress on the knee, causing damage to the collateral and cruciate ligaments.
- **Muscle injuries** The muscles can be overloaded, resulting in muscle tears or ruptures. Direct blows to the muscle can cause haematoma (bleeding and bruising) within the muscle.
- **Injuries to tendons** In situations where explosive forces are applied – as in take-offs – the tendons may be ruptured. The most common are ruptures to the biceps and Achilles tendons.
- **Bone injuries** Collisions with the apparatus, repetitive impact loads or falls may result in fractures (or stress fractures) to the bones.

Overuse Injuries
These injuries are more frequently experienced by adolescents during the pubescent growth periods and are generally associated with:
- Inadequate levels of fitness

- Poor technique
- Muscle imbalance
- Excessive repetitive loading
- Unsuitable apparatus or landing mats.

The areas of the body most at risk are:
- **The wrist** Repetitive rotation and compression loading can cause damage to the growth plates.
- **The knee** The strong repetitive contractions of the quadriceps in running, take-off and landings pull on the patella ligament just below the knee. This results in tenderness and bone damage just below the knee in an injury called Osgood Schlatter's disease.
- **The ankle** Repetitive running and jumping places stress on the attachment of the Achilles tendon on the heel and this may result in fragments of bone being torn from the heel. This overuse injury is called Severs disease.
- **The elbow** Tenderness at the point of attachment of the ligament.
- **The tendons** Inflammation of the tendons in wrist, forearm and Achilles tendon, causing tenderness and classified as tendonitis.
- **The load-bearing bones** Frequent, repetitive loading may bring on small, often difficult to locate, stress fractures within the bones.

The symptoms of an overuse injury are the gradual onset of pain during and after activity, resulting in the pain preventing training. There is often very little evidence of swelling in the area of tenderness.

Treatment and Management of Injuries

As part of their duty of care, all coaches should minimize the risk of injury through meticulous planning of the training and by following good coaching practice. Careful planning of the training load is vital, following safe, progressive learning principles, while perfecting the correct technique will also reduce the risk of injury. The coach must be swift to spot the onset of fatigue and sensitive to the development of pain, weakness, lack of endurance and illness.

The gymnast is subject to great external forces in the giant swing on rings.

- **Protect** the injury from further damage.
- **Rest** the affected area.
- **Ice** the injured area for not more than 6–8 minutes every 2–4 hours for 24–36 hours.
- **Compress** the area by applying a compression bandage (not taping) between icing to reduce swelling.
- **Elevate** the injured limb to control the blood flow.
- **Refer** the injured person to a medical person such as a doctor or physiotherapist.

Rehabilitation

After an injury has occurred and a medically qualified person has cleared the gymnast to return to training, the coach should work with the gymnast to ensure their safe return. The coach should respect and adhere to the advice provided by the doctor or physiotherapist.

The following programme is designed to facilitate the rehabilitation of the gymnast:
1. Restore the range of movement in the injured part.
2. Regain the flexibility in other areas where this may have been lost through immobility during the period of the injury.
3. Develop the strength and restore confidence in the recovering parts of the body.
4. Regain co-ordination and balance.
5. Gradually reintroduce the gymnastic skills.

The physiotherapist may recommend that the injured part be protected or supported by means of strapping until full strength and confidence is restored.

The author and publisher hope that you have found this book to be both informative and interesting. Gymnastics is a participant-centred sport with high moral and ethical values. It is family oriented and is concerned with the holistic development of the gymnasts no matter what their level of participation is. Hopefully the book may have inspired you to become involved in the sport as a gymnast, coach, official or supportive parent. If so we hope that you enjoy your participation and find it to be rewarding.

During periods of adolescent growth spurt the coach needs to be particularly attentive to physical changes in the body, amending the training programme accordingly to safeguard the young gymnasts.

The coach also has a responsibility to manage any injury appropriately to minimize the trauma. In the event of a suspected serious injury the coach must stop the class and immediately seek emergency medical support. The injured person should not be moved until it is confirmed by a medically trained person that it is safe to do so. Emergency first aid may be applied by a suitably trained person where this necessary.

For less serious, soft-tissue injuries immediate first aid may be applied and this should follow the PRICER sequence:

GLOSSARY

This is a glossary of terms and words used in this book and in gymnastics generally. The gymnastics usage of a term given here may differ from a dictionary definition.

Accelerator A gymnastic skill that is used to increase the speed of movement

Acrobatic elements Gymnastic movements, which include somersaults, back flips and handsprings

Adenosine triphosphate The immediately usable form of energy stored in the muscles and liver

Aerobic exercise Exercise that requires oxygen to release the energy stored in the muscles and liver

All-around A competition in which the gymnast competes on all the apparatus

Anaerobic exercise Exercise that does not require oxygen to release the stored energy

Arch A body shape in which the spine is bent backwards

Back flip A backwards handspring

Body shape The posture shown by the gymnast, such as tuck, stretch, dish or arch

Body tension Holding the mid-body tight to control the shape of the body

Burnout An effect of fatigue causing under-performance

Calorific intake The total number of calories contained in the food we eat

Carbohydrates The main source of energy in food

Choreography The arrangement of body movements and dance elements in a floor or beam routine

Consistency Being able to repeat a movement or skill accurately over and over

Consolidation period Time spent in training to ensure consistency in performing a skill or movement

Cool-down A series of light exercises used to commence recovery after training

Dedication Being fully committed to something

Dietician A person trained to advise on the content of the diet

Difficulty value The numerical figure used to indicate the level of difficulty of a movement or skill

Dish A body shape in which the body is slightly concave

Dismount A movement used to end the routine, departing the apparatus and landing on the floor

Double somersault Two complete rotations of the body around the horizontal axis

Dynamic Powerful and fast (movement or action)

Element An individual gymnastic skill or movement

Endo circle A forwards straddle circle finishing in handstand on the asymmetric bars or horizontal bar

Endurance The ability to repeatedly perform physical exercises for some time before tiring

Extrinsic motivation The use of external rewards to motivate the gymnast

Flexibility The range of movement in a joint complex

Focus To concentrate attention on something

Giant swing A complete rotation around the bar with the body extended in the handstand shape

Gienger salto A backwards somersault with one half-turn to re-grasp the bar

Goals Aims, targets or ambitions

Hand guard or hand grip A leather strap worn on the hands to provide a grip on the apparatus and to protect the hands against wear due to friction

Intrinsic motivation Self-motivation, or motivation from within oneself

Joint The point in the skeleton where two bones meet

Judges Officials who assess and score the gymnast's performance

Mental preparation Using training methods to visualize a movement pattern or learn how to deal with nervousness or stress

Momentum The degree of motion gained as a result of movement. The faster a body moves the more momentum it will possess

Morale The level of confidence and spirit a gymnast has

Multiple twists More than one turn around the long axis of the body

Muscle The parts of the body which contract to cause a limb or bones to move

Nutrition The process through which the body gains benefits from the food and drink we digest

Nutritionist A person who is trained to provide advice on the food we should eat

Olympian A person who has competed at an Olympic Games

Optional exercises A sequence of voluntary gymnastic skills performed by a gymnast in a routine

Peaking Increasing the training load to a maximum at a particular point in the training programme

Physiotherapist A person who is trained to prevent injury or help you to recover from injury

Pike A body shape in which the body is folded forward at the hips

Planche A gymnastic skill in which the body is held horizontally, supported only by the arms and hands

Positive self-talk The practice of reciting positive statements to eliminate negative thoughts

Posture The shape in which the body is held

Proprioceptive imagery Visually rehearsing a movement in your mind

Protein A nutrient in our food, which is used to repair body tissue

Psychologist A person who is trained to teach others how to mentally prepare or cope with stress

Psychology The science in which the function of the mind is studied and used to train the mind

Pubescent growth period The period of rapid growth in young people

Ranking The order in which a gymnast or team is placed according to their scores

Rebound Movements that occur as a result of repulsion from an apparatus such as a springboard, trampette or trampoline

Rehabilitation The period of recovery following injury or illness

Release and re-catch A gymnastic skill in which the gymnast releases the grasp on the bar, somersaults and re-catches the bar

Resistance How difficult it is to move something

Rotation A movement in which the body turns about an axis

Routine A sequence of gymnastic skills performed in a competition. Often called the 'competition exercise'

Scissors or shear A pommel horse skill in which the gymnast swings with straddled legs and undercuts one leg under the other

Self-evaluation Reflecting on and evaluating your own performance

Soft tissue Muscles, tendons and ligaments in the body

Spatial awareness The ability to orientate oneself whilst somersaulting or twisting

Special requirement A specified type of gymnastic movement that must be included in a routine

Spotting Physical support provided by a coach or partner

Stalder circle A straddle circle backwards into handstand on the bar

Stamina Ability to do a physical activity for a long time

Start value The value of a routine before points are deducted

Static Not moving

Straddle A position in which the legs are wide apart

Tapering Gradually reducing the training load just prior to a competition

Tariff The value awarded to a vault or skill according to its level of difficulty

Thomas flair An element on pommel horse in which the gymnast circles with their legs in splits

Tkatchev A release and re-catch element involving a straddle backwards over the bar

Tuck A position in which the legs are bent and the knees are pulled into the chest

Twist A turn around the long axis of the body during the performance of a somersault

Uneven bars Another term for asymmetric bars

Value parts Each gymnastic skill is awarded a value according to its difficulty and graded A, B, C, D, E or F

Vitamins Nutrients in the food, which are used to assist in the metabolism of food

Warm-up Performing a series of light exercises to warm up the body and muscles prior to the training session

USEFUL CONTACTS AND ADDRESSES

Below are some useful contacts for information on gymnastics, including details for gymnastics governing bodies and other relevant organizations.

Fédération Internationale de Gymnastique (FIG)
Website: www.fig-gymnastics.com
Email: info@fig-gymnastics.org

British Gymnastics
Website: www.british-gymnstics.org
Email: information@british-gymnastics.org

English Gymnastics
Website: www.englandgymnastics.org.uk
Email: information@englishgymnastics.org.uk

Northern Ireland Gymnastics
Website: www.northernirelandgymnastics.com
Email: nigymnastics@btopenworld.com

Scottish Gymnastics
Website: www.scottishgymnastics.com
Email: info@scottishgymnastics.org

Welsh Gymnastics
Website: www.welshgymnastics.org
Email: office@welshgymnastics.org

USA Gymnastics
Website: www.usa-gymnastics.org
Email: membership@usagymnastics.org

Australia Gymnastics
Website: www.gymnastics.org.au
Email: ausgym@gymnastics.org.au

Sports Coach UK
Website: www.sportscoachuk.org
Email: enquiries@coachwise.ltd.org

INDEX